HOW TO WIN AT CHESS

Other titles for the beginner include:

Starting Out in Chess
Byron Jacobs

Tips for Young Players
Matthew Sadler

Learn Chess: A Complete Course
Alexander & Beech

Basic Chess Openings
Gabor Kallai

Improve Your Chess Now
Jonathan Tisdall

Choose the Right Move
Daniel King and Chris Duncan

First Steps in Chess
John Walker

Chess Fundamentals
José Capablanca

Test Your Chess: Piece Power
John Walker

HOW TO WIN AT CHESS

10 GOLDEN RULES TO FOLLOW

Daniel King

EVERYMAN CHESS

Everyman Chess, formerly Cadogan Chess,
is published by Everyman Publishers, London

Everyman Chess

Distributed in North America by The Globe Pequot Press, 246 Goose Lane, PO Box 480, Guilford, CT 06437-0480

All other sales enquiries should be directed to Everyman Chess, Gloucester Mansions, 140A Shaftesbury Avenue, London, WC2H 8HD
Email: dan@everyman.uk.com
Website: www.everyman.uk.com

First edition published 1995 by Cadogan Books plc, 27-29 Berwick St., London W1V 3RF
Reprinted 1997, 1998, 1999, 2001, 2002, 2003

British Library Cataloguing in Publication Data
A CIP catalogue record for this book is available from the British Library.

ISBN 1 85744 072 2

Cover design by Brian Robins
Typeset by ChessSetter
Printed and bound in Great Britain by
The Bath Press, Bath

Contents

Part One: Opening the Game

Part Two: The Middlegame

Part Three: The Endgame

Introduction

If you have just learned the moves and would like some guidance as to what you should be aiming for, then this is the book for you. Alternatively, if you have already been playing for some time, but would like to consolidate your knowledge, then you are also at the right place.

I have sought to pin down ten of the most important principles to bear in mind during the game: three for the opening; four for the middlegame; and three for the endgame.

At first, especially on the page, these rules might appear abstract, but the more you play, the more you will appreciate their relevance. For the top players in the world who have a wealth of experience, these principles now come as second nature, and it is this that they rely upon rather than any supposed ability to memorise strings of long variations. I am not pretending that simply by reading this book you will join the world's elite – that only comes through years of practice – but it will give you a solid foundation from which you can be confident of improving your game.

I would recommend that you go through each rule carefully rather than attempt to polish off the whole book in an evening; that way they are more likely to stick. I don't know about you, but I find that trying to keep ten things in mind at the same time is a chancy business.

Note that I write above that these are rules to 'bear in mind'. I am not advocating that you follow them slavishly: if you get into a situation where the rule says 'get castled', but you see a way to capture your opponent's queen, then don't hesitate, whip it off!

If you are unfamiliar with chess notation, then I would strongly recommend that you take a look at the next section 'Understanding chess notation' before moving on to the bulk of the book. Don't be put off by this, it is very simple; and there will be plenty of diagrams throughout the book to help you along.

Just to emphasise again, there is no substitute for practice. The more you play, the more you will understand and the better you will play, but if you keep these ten rules in mind, you will be heading in the right direction.

Daniel King, London, August 1995

Understanding chess notation

Compared to other games, chess is fortunate in that there is a simple method of recording moves, enabling us to play through games from the greatest players in the world, not just from recent times, but from centuries ago. In view of this, it is hardly surprising that there is such a large body of chess literature, ranging from monthly magazines with the latest games and information, to games collections by the greatest players, to theoretical manuals on the most fashionable opening variations. Once you have learnt the notation all of this is open to you.

Although much of this book can be read from the page simply by looking at the diagrams, you will get more out of it if you develop a grasp of chess notation.

The system of recording moves used almost exclusively around the world is known as 'algebraic notation'. Thankfully it is not as complicated as it sounds. If you have ever played the game of 'battleships', or are able to negotiate the grid system of a city street plan, then understanding chess notation will come easily to you.

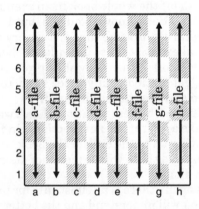

The rows of squares up the board are each given a letter (a to h) and are known as files (see diagram); the rows of squares across the board are known as ranks and are given a number. Thus each square has its own 'name'.

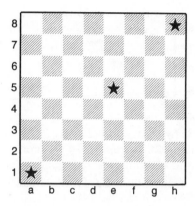

The square in the bottom left hand corner with the star is 'a1'; the square in the top right hand corner with the star is 'h8'; the star in the centre is 'e5'.

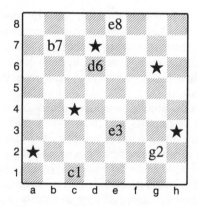

Some of the squares in the above diagram have been marked with their correct notation, others have been marked with a star. To make sure that you have understood the system correctly, identify the starred squares. (Solutions on page 123.)

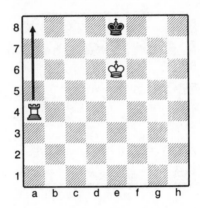

In this position White is able to give checkmate by moving his rook to the a8 square. This move would be recorded as:

1 ♖a8 checkmate

The '1' at the front of the move indicates the move number, in this case the first move after the diagram; the '♖' represents the rook; and 'a8' is the square the rook is moving to (note, in standard notation, only the square the piece moves to is recorded, not where it has come from); and the checkmate is self-explanatory! (Sometimes checkmate is abbreviated simply to 'mate'.)

Each piece on the board is represented by a letter: king=K; queen=Q; rook=R; bishop=B; knight=N (to avoid confusion with the king); the pawn is not given a letter, simply the square it moves to is recorded. However, in most books figurines are used for the pieces instead of initials, i.e. king=♔; queen=♕; rook=♖; bishop=♗; knight=♘.

If a piece is captured, it is recorded with a lower case 'x'; thus, ♗xc6, would mean that a bishop captured a piece that was standing on the c6 square.

Starting from the next diagram, try playing through the following moves on your own chessboard.

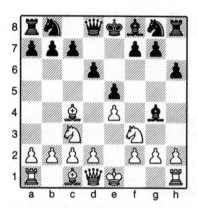

1	♘xe5	♗xd1
2	♗xf7+	♔e7
3	♘d5 checkmate	

With a bit of luck, you will have reached the position in the following diagram.

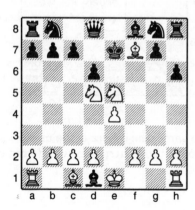

Part One: Opening the game

Introduction

In chess, the opening moves are critical; get those wrong and you could be doomed. It is worth thinking about what our aims should be at the start of the game. Checkmate is the ultimate goal, but just how is that to be achieved? Should we hang back with our pieces, waiting for the right moment to strike? Or creep around the edges of the board, hoping to carry out a guerrilla raid?

I would not recommend either of these two strategies. Chess is a war game. Think of the board as a battlefield with two armies opposing each other. Which part of the board is going to be the most important?

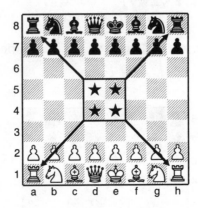

At the start of the game, the centre is the most important part of the board. If you dominate the centre you will dominate the rest of the board.

51

Look for captures

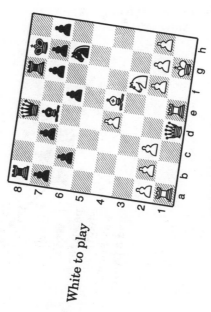

White to play

Black to play

Solutions

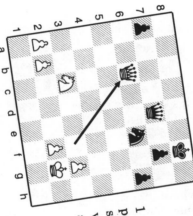

1 ♕xc6. The queen captures the pawn for free. Taking the knight instead would have been disastrous – it was securely protected by a queen and a pawn.

There are no good captures here. It would be a mistake to capture the knight as the rook would be recaptured by the pawn. As the rook is worth five points and the knight only three, Black would lose out.

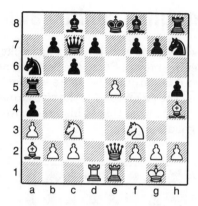

Look at the above position, which side would you rather play, White's or Black's?

White has a dominating central position. The pawn on e5 acts as a spearhead for White's attack, effectively cutting Black's position in two. The bishops, though at the side of the board, are actually well placed, slicing across Black's king. The knights also stand well, ready to leap into aggressive positions. The rooks bear down on Black's king. White's queen is also poised to strike.

Compare this with Black's position. He has lost the opening battle, having been unable to place a pawn in the centre and thereby give cover for some of his pieces. Instead he has been forced to bring out his pieces at the side of the board where they have little influence over the play. The bishops are still on their starting squares, one of them blocked in completely by pawns. The rooks and knights are stuck out on the edge. Worst of all, Black's king is caught in the centre, in the line of fire of White's pieces. (Compare it with White's king tucked away safely at the side of the board behind a fence of pawns.)

Here, White has several promising moves, but there is one in particular which is quite devastating. Can you find it? (Solution on page 123.)

The first three Golden Rules are closely interlinked. Following them will help you to avoid falling into a position as desperate as Black's in the above example, and, more positively, they will explain how to go about building a position as imposing as White's.

Rule 1: Open with a centre pawn

White always begins the game and, initially, has a choice of no less than twenty different opening moves. Some are better than others.

I would recommend beginning the game by moving one of the two centre pawns. Playing the pawn to e4 is the classic opening move (1 e4). Every world champion has used this as his first move at one time or another, so you are in good company.

The pawn occupies one of the four central squares, and controls another.

In addition, the diagonal path of the bishop and queen are opened up.

Moving the pawn to d4 on the first move is also strong. As is the case with 1 e4, the pawn occupies one of the four central squares and controls another. As well as that, the bishop on c1 is now free to move.

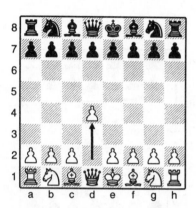

If you were playing Black, which of the following four moves would you choose?

(a) 1...e5 (b) 1...a5 (c) 1...♘c6 (d) 1...d5

Let's consider each move in turn.

(a) 1...e5

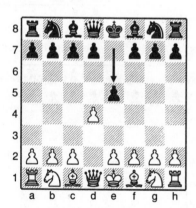

It is true, the general rule is 'open with a centre pawn', but in this specific case Black simply loses a pawn to 2 dxe5.

(b) 1...a5

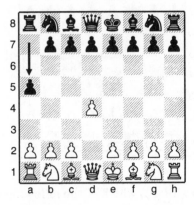

So you wanted to bring out your rook at the side of the board? No chance. White simply replies 2 e4, preventing the rook from advancing to a6 (there's a bishop covering the square) and establishes a dominating central position. Black's pawn move contributes nothing to the struggle for the centre.

(c) 1...♘c6

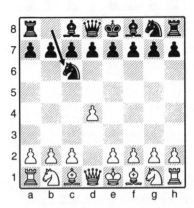

A risky move. Since the black knight lacks pawn cover, it may be driven away by 2 d5. The knight is attacked and must therefore move again, so Black loses precious time.

(d) 1...d5

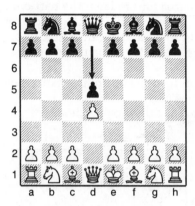

A good move, and by far the best of the options above. Black gains ground in the centre and opens up the line of one of his bishops.

To conclude, it is important to open with a centre pawn:

1. In order to mark out territory in the centre of the board.
2. To clear the path for one of the bishops to enter the game.

Rule 2: Bring out your pieces

Just as it would be foolish for the commander of an army to leave his forces back in the barracks, so it would be unwise to leave your pieces on their starting squares for too long: the battle might be over before they even get a chance to march onto the field. It is vital to bring out your knights, bishops, rooks and queen as quickly as possible. But don't just use one or two pieces, try to bring as many as possible into the game.

Set up the position for the start of the game, and then play the following two moves: 1 e4 c5.

That brings you to the following position.

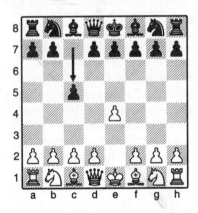

Both of these moves are sensible: they each control one of the four central squares. But how would you continue with White now? Consider the following four moves. Which would you choose to play?

(a) 2 h4 (b) 2 ♘f3 (c) 2 ♘h3 (d) 2 ♕h5

(a) 2 h4

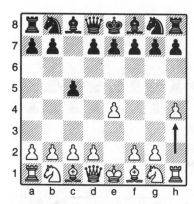

A dreadful move. Pawn moves should only be made in the opening to win space in the centre, or to enable a piece to be developed. It would not be a good idea to bring the rook out at the side of the board: it will become too exposed.

(b) 2 ♘f3

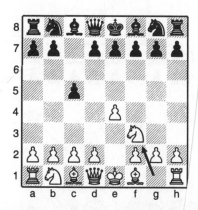

The best of the four moves. From the
of the four cen

knights before the bishops: it is not quite clear where the bishop would be best placed at the moment, but it is certain that the knight belongs on this square.

(c) 2 ♘h3

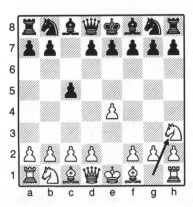

Not as strong as playing the knight to f3. From the side of the board the knight has less influence over the centre.

(d) 2 ♕h5

board, but without the support of its army it can achieve very little.

The queen attacks the pawn on c5 but this can be defended easily, for instance by advancing the pawn to e6. Now it would be unwise to capture the pawn...

Each piece on the board has a rough material value (see table).

So you can see how important it is to take good care of your queen.

On the next move the queen will be driven away by the knight or the pawn and White will have lost valuable time.

Values of the pieces	
queen	= 9 points
rook	= 5 points
knight	= 3 points
bishop	= 3 points
pawn	= 1 point

It is best to bring out your knights and bishops first, which will enable you to castle as quickly as possible. The queen is normally only brought out to an attacking position when it is clear that it will not come under fire itself.

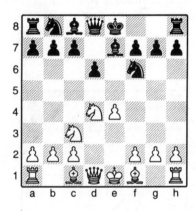

In this position it is White to move. What would you play?
(a) 1 h3 (b) 1 ♗c4 (c) 1 ♗b5+ (d) 1 ♕f3

(a) 1 h3

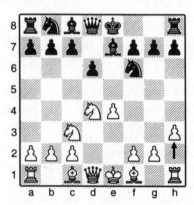

Not good. Only move a pawn in the opening if it helps you to win space in the centre, or if it enables you to bring out your pieces. This move just wastes time.

(b) 1 &c4

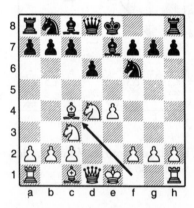

The strongest of the four moves. The bishop positions itself on an excellent diagonal cutting down towards Black's king, and White prepares castling – more on this in the next chapter.

(c) 1 ♗b5+

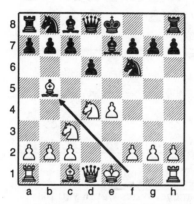

The check doesn't actually achieve anything. Black simply blocks with ...c6. The bishop is attacked and must now retreat.

(d) 1 ♕f3

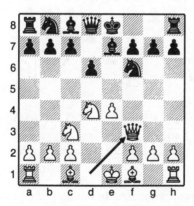

Bringing the queen out at such an early stage is inadvisable. It is liable to be attacked by Black's pieces, and time will have been lost.

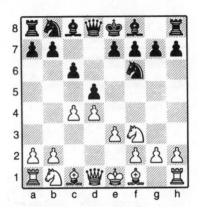

Here it is Black's move. What would you play?
(a) 1...e6 (b) 1...dxc4 (c) 1...♛a5+ (d) 1...♞e4

(a) 1...e6

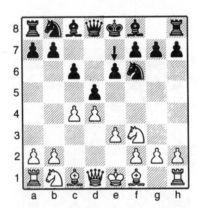

This is a good move, preparing to develop the bishop and then bring the king to safety.

(b) 1...dxc4

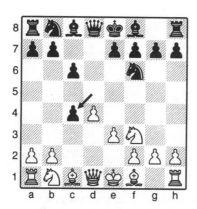

Capturing this pawn isn't too bad, the problem is that it helps White to develop. White will simply recapture, ♗xc4, and the bishop stands well. The trade has not helped Black to bring out any of his pieces.

(c) 1...♕a5+

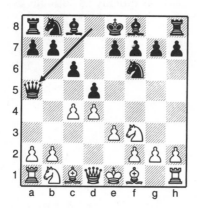

A poor move. Just because it is check, this doesn't mean that the move is strong. White blocks the check with 2 ♗d2, and the queen must retreat straight away.

(d) 1...♘e4

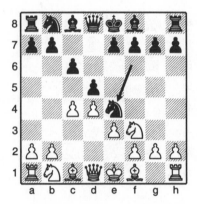

Not the best move. This knight should not be allowed to hog the action. In the opening, it is best to move each piece just once, unless you have a very good reason, otherwise you will never manage to bring out your whole army.

When bringing out your pieces, it is important to remember that you should be aiming to castle as quickly as possible. See Rule 3!

Rule 3: Castle as quickly as possible

At the start of the game, a raging battle will take place for the centre to decide who will dominate the board.

While the king is your most precious piece – if it gets checkmated you will lose the game – at the same time it is also one of your least powerful men. It can in no way contribute to the struggle for the centre in the opening and should escape to the side of the board as soon as possible. This is when it pays to know about the special rule in chess known as *castling*.

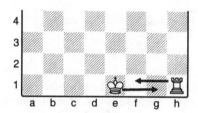

If neither king nor rook have moved from their starting squares, then it is possible to castle. The king always moves two squares and the rook then leaps over and next to it. This is all done in one move.

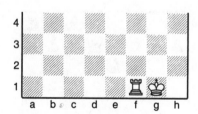

Castling on this side of the board is known as 'short castling', or perhaps more correctly 'kingside castling'. This is recorded in chess notation as 0-0.

It is also possible to castle on the other side of the board. This is known as 'long castling' or 'queenside castling'.

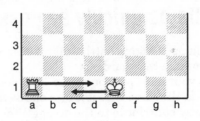

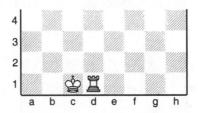

This is recorded in chess notation as 0-0-0.

The importance of castling cannot be stressed enough. It enables you to get your king to safety at the side of the board, and at the same time to bring your rook into a position from where it can influence the centre. Let's look at a couple of situations that show how useful it can be to castle.

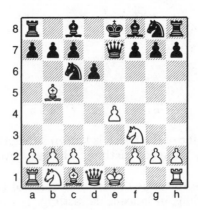

Black has just played 1...♕e7, attacking the white pawn in the middle of the board. Instead of defending the pawn directly, White simply castled (2 0-0).

If Black now takes the pawn with 2...♕xe4, then White is able to win Black's queen. How? (Solution on page 123.)

When I first began to play chess, my hero was the American world champion Bobby Fischer. There was a particular opening variation of his that I used to great effect; it involves a similar trap to the previous example:

1   e4   e5

Both players bring out their pawns into the centre of the board in classical fashion.

2   ♘f3

The knight is brought out (or 'developed' to use the chess jargon) to a good square, influencing the centre, and attacking a pawn.

2   ...   ♘c6

A good move. Black had to defend the pawn, and does so by bringing out a knight.

3   ♗b5

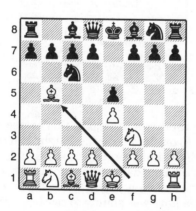

This opening is known as the 'Ruy Lopez' (or simply the 'Spanish') Opening after a 16th century Spanish priest named Ruy Lopez de Segura, one of the leading players of that era. It is still one of the most popular openings used today. (Ruy Lopez's other most notable contribution to the game was his recommendation that one should place the

board so that the sun shines in your opponent's eyes, though I have re-
frained from including this as one of my Golden Rules.)

The white bishop (appropriately enough) puts pressure on the knight
which is defending the central pawn.

3   ...   a6

Black calls White's bluff and demands to know the bishop's inten-
tion. It was also possible to bring out a piece with 3...♘f6 or 3...♗c5.

4   ♗xc6

This was the idea that Fischer made fashionable. It is also perfectly
possible to retreat the bishop with 4 ♗a4.

4   ...   dxc6

Black recaptures the bishop. It is an equal exchange: White has given
up the bishop, worth three points, for a knight, also worth three points.

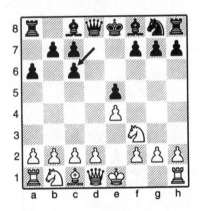

Here White could capture a pawn, but this course of action would be
inadvisable: after 5 ♘xe5 ♕d4 both the knight and the pawn would be
threatened and once the knight retreats, say 6 ♘f3, then Black replies
6...♕xe4+, and White's king has been caught in the middle. Remember,
the king should be tucked away safely at the side of the board. For that
reason Fischer's idea here was simply to castle, getting his king out of
the centre before embarking on any adventures:

5   0-0

Now Black's pawn in the middle really is threatened (6 ♘xe5 ♕d4 7
♘f3 ♕xe4 8 ♖e1 wins the queen). There are various ways for Black to
defend his 'e'-pawn, for example 5...♗d6; 5...f6 and, the sneakiest,
5...♗g4 (see the section on 'pins' later on in *Rule 6: Look out for tactics*).

However, some of my opponents preferred counter-attack to defence – normally a good policy, but here a mistake – by playing the move...

5   ...   ♘f6

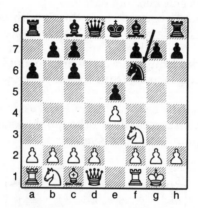

Not terribly clever. For after...

5   ♘xe5   ♘xe4
6   ♖e1

...the rook enters the game with deadly effect. Black has been caught in a trap, for if the knight retreats...

6   ...   ♘f6

...then White has a decisive coup:

7   ♘xc6+

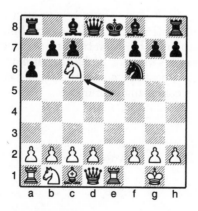

This opens up a check from the rook towards the black king, while at the same time White's knight threatens the queen. Black *must* get out of check with, say, 7...♝e6, leaving White to swipe off the queen with 8 ♞xd8, which will be enough to win the game. This is a typical scenario in the opening if one side does not castle.

Notice in the above sequence how the first three rules are interlinked. *Open with a centre pawn* (Rule 1) gave White some control over the centre and enabled the bishop to be developed (Rule 2: *Bring out your pieces*); and then bringing out the bishop and knight cleared the way for the white king to *castle* (Rule 3), enabling the rook to come into the centre.

There are certain instances when although the king and rook are still on their starting squares, castling is not possible.

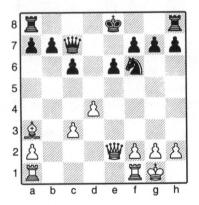

It is Black's move. Castling short is illegal in this position as Black's king is not allowed to move through the line of the bishop standing on a3. However, it is still possible for Black to castle on the queenside. Indeed, that would be the best move, evacuating the king from the centre of the board before it comes to any harm.

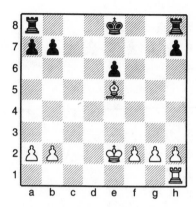

Can Black castle (a) long (b) short (c) on both sides (d) not at all?

In fact it is possible to castle on either side of the board. Although the white bishop cuts through to one of the rooks in the corner, and across the path of the other, it is still legal for Black to castle. Crucially, Black's king is still free to move; if the king is in check then castling is illegal.

I would actually prefer to castle on the kingside as then White would be unable to capture the rook in the corner.

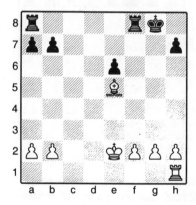

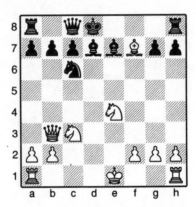

In this position it is White to play. The queen, knights and bishop are all in strong attacking positions, but the king is still in the centre of the board and the rooks are stuck out at the edges. The obvious solution to these problems would be for White to castle, but on which side?

Should White castle (a) long or (b) short?

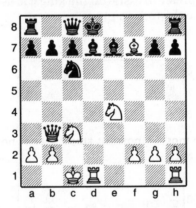

Without doubt, the best move is to castle long.

The rook in the corner has moved to the centre of the board and now faces Black's king. Although a bishop stands in the way, it will not be long before White batters through and the black king will have nowhere to escape to.

There is one game which I always think of when describing these first three rules. Once again I'm turning to Bobby Fischer to show us the way. It was played in an off-hand game, and shows the former world champion's great instinct for attack.

R. Fischer – R. Fine
New York 1963

1 e4

Fischer used this as his first move almost exclusively throughout his career. To reiterate, opening with a centre pawn enables you to gain ground in the middle of the board, and prepares the development of one of the bishops.

1 ... e5

Black follows suit. Be careful about attempting to copy your opponent indefinitely though, as this can quickly lead to disaster for the second player. More on this later.

2 ♘f3

We have already seen this move: the knight enters the game and at the same time attacks a pawn.

2 ... ♘c6

Black brings out a knight and defends the pawn. If White's knight were now to capture the pawn with 3 ♘xe5, then Black's knight would hack it off with 3...♘xe5: Black has gained three points, but White only one, evidently a poor exchange.

Instead, Fischer brings out his bishop.

3 ♗c4

In the example I gave earlier, we looked at the move 3 ♗b5 – the Spanish Opening. The alternative development of the bishop to c4 is just as valid, and it simply isn't possible to say that one move is better than the other. The most important thing is that both conform to our rule: a piece is brought out to a square where it is able to influence the centre.

3 ... ♗c5

Black plays in similar fashion.

At this point, White has many reasonable moves, for instance, 4 ♘c3, bringing a piece into the centre; 4 d3, preparing to develop the other bishop; or simply 4 0-0, removing the king from the centre.

Instead of these, Fischer selects a more dynamic continuation: he chooses to sacrifice a pawn, and in return, speeds up his development.

4 b4

If you think that Black may simply take this pawn off, then congratulations, you are right; however, the situation is not quite as clear as it looks at first glance.

The move 4 b4 in this position is known as the 'Evans Gambit' after an English sea captain, W.D.Evans, who first recommended it as long ago as 1824. It isn't as old-fashioned as it sounds, though: recently world champion Garry Kasparov won a couple of beautiful games with this gambit.

> **What's a Gambit?**
>
> A 'gambit' is the sacrifice of a pawn, or sometimes even a piece, during the opening phase of the game, in order to gain some other advantage in return. Gambits are notoriously tricky: everyone likes to take pieces, but few think about the consequences thereafter. The word derives from the 16th century Italian slang, 'gambetta', originally used in the sport of wrestling, meaning 'to set a trap'. ('Gamba' means leg, so presumably it involved tripping the opponent up in some way.)

4   ...   ♗xb4

Pawn number one is grabbed by Black.

5   c3

The pawn attacks the bishop, forcing it to retreat.

5   ...   ♗a5

6   d4

No messing around. Fischer charges his pawn forward in the centre, opening up lines for his pieces.

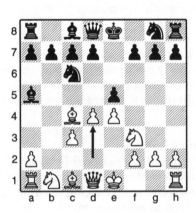

6   ...   exd4

Black grabs pawn number two: be careful, what about our first three rules?

7   0-0

It wasn't possible for White to recapture the pawn as his king would have been in check from the bishop; in other words, the recapture was illegal. Instead, Fischer just calmly removes his king from the centre. Rule 3, *get castled quickly* has been achieved, and this turns out to be one of the deciding factors in this game.

7   ...   dxc3

This is pure greed: Black takes pawn number three, flagrantly flouting the Golden Rules. What about developing some pieces? What about castling? Black must pay for such recklessness.

8   ♕b3

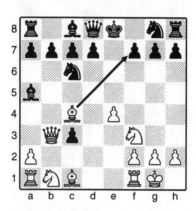

The attack starts here. White brings the queen out to a safe square forming a battery with the bishop; the threat is 9 ♗xf7+ wrecking Black's king position. (Remember, if the black king moves then it cannot castle, and will therefore be unable to escape from an attack down the middle of the board.)

8   ...   ♕e7

The queen defends the pawn. If White were now to capture the pawn with the bishop, 9 ♗xf7+, then he would lose material after 9...♕xf7. (Work it through for yourself if you are not sure.)

9   ♘xc3

One of the sacrificed pawns is recaptured, and at the same time the knight enters the battle. Naturally the knight can be captured by the bishop, 9...♝xc3, but the queen simply recaptures, 10 ♛xc3, threatening the pawn on g7, and the attack would continue.

9   ...   ♞f6

Black finally brings out his knight and prepares to castle, but it is too late.

10   ♞d5

White uses the fact that he has brought out more of his pieces than Black to initiate a deadly attack.

Black must deal with the threat to the queen from the knight and therefore exchanges it off.

10   ...   ♞xd5

11   exd5

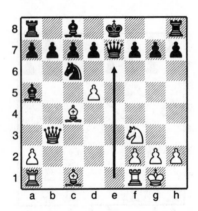

The pawn now attacks the other knight, forcing it to move, and (this is the clever bit) opens up the file in front of Black's king.

11   ...   ♞e5

12   ♞xe5   ♛xe5

Seemingly an equal exchange as both sides gave away a knight, but in fact this was more desirable for White as he has dragged the black queen into the centre of the board where it now becomes a target.

13   ♝b2

The bishop enters the game by attacking the queen.

13   ...   ♛g5

Just compare the two positions. White has developed both bishops and his queen, his king is castled, hidden away safely at the side of the board, and the rooks are ready to enter the game. Black, on the other hand, has a few more difficulties. The only pieces he has developed are his queen and bishop, and, crucially, his king is still in the middle of the board. If it were his move, then the picture wouldn't look so gloomy: by castling here, Black would solve many of the problems of his position, and after all, he does have two extra pawns.

However, it is White to move and Fischer conceives of a clever way to trap the black king in the centre of the board. In the opening, timing is everything.

14 h4

Giving up yet another pawn, though Fischer gets it back straight away.

14 ... ♛xh4
15 ♗xg7

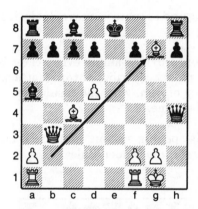

This is the point. The bishop captures the pawn and attacks the rook, forcing it to move; once the rook moves it is no longer possible for the king to castle so Black's monarch is now at the mercy of the white pieces.

15 ... ♖g8
16 ♖fe1+ ♚d8

It was possible to play 16...♗xe1, but the finale after 17 ♖xe1+ would have been exactly the same. You can see from this how important it is to connect the rooks so that they are protecting each other. This can only be done if you castle (Rule 3!) and bring out the rest of your pieces (Rule 2!!).

17 ♛g3

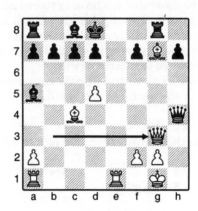

Here **Black resigned** as mate is unavoidable: if 17...♛xg3, then 18 ♗f6 is mate.

The final position provides ample evidence of White's successful strategy: all of his pieces contributed to the attack, whereas Black's greed got the better of him, with the result that some of his pieces didn't even enter the game.

To round off this opening section, here are some positions to test your grasp of the first three Golden Rules.

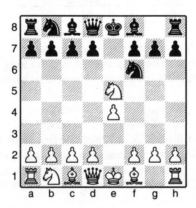

Question: Would it be sensible for Black to continue copying White's moves with 3...♘xe4 here?

Answer: No. A strategy of copying one's opponent almost always leads to disaster, and this is a classic case.

If White plays 4 ♕e2, then Black is already in big trouble. If the knight retreats by 4...♘f6, then 5 ♘c6+ wins Black's queen – we have already seen this 'discovered check' motif earlier on.

Continuing the copy-cat strategy also doesn't improve matters: 4 ♕e2 ♕e7 5 ♕xe4, and now maintaining the symmetry would be inadvisable.

Defending the knight after 4 ♕e2 would not avoid trouble: 4...d5 5 d3, and if the knight moves, then 6 ♘c6+ still wins the queen.

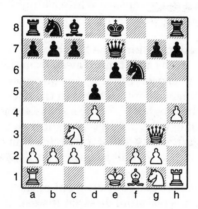

Question: Would Black be well advised to lunge forward with 1...♘e4 in this position?

Answer: Definitely not. It is true that White's queen is attacked, but this can be dealt with very easily by playing 2 ♘xe4 dxe4, and now if White simply castles on the queenside, 3 0-0-0, then his king is safe and he has a good game.

Unless one has a very good reason, do not move a piece twice early on in the game. Time is of the essence in the opening.

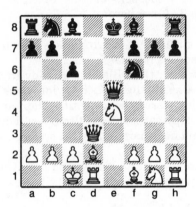

Question: Should Black capture White's knight in the centre of the board, (a) with the queen or (b) with the knight?

Answer: Ha! Neither. Taking the knight with the queen (1...♕xe4) loses to 2 ♖e1. The queen cannot move away from the rook's attack as it would put the king in check. 'Pinning' the queen against the king with the rook is an extremely common theme in the opening.

Capturing with the knight (1...♘xe4) also loses, though in a more unusual and spectacular way: 2 ♕d8+ is a shocker of a queen sacrifice which forces mate after 2...♔xd8 3 ♗g5+ (double check from bishop and rook) and now 3...♔c7 4 ♗d8 is mate; as is 3...♔e8 4 ♖d8 mate.

The moral of this is to get your king out of the centre as quickly as possible to avoid such a potential disaster. Instead of taking the knight, a simple developing move such as 1...♗e7, preparing to castle, would be acceptable.

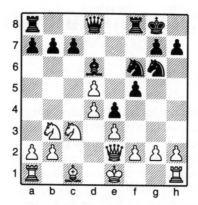

Question: It is White to play. Is it advisable to castle in this position?

Answer: No. In most cases, castling is correct, but here it would be a mistake. Take a look at Black's pieces clustered around the sector of the board where White's king would land – they are queuing up to take a shot.

In fact after 1 0-0, Black would crash through straight away with the deadly piece sacrifice 1...♗xh2+. After 2 ♔xh2 ♘g4+, the king is mated if it moves up the board, 3 ♔g3 ♛h4 mate; and if it moves backwards, 3 ♔g1 ♛h4 will also lead to a quick conclusion; Black's immediate threat is 4...♛h2, and after 4 ♖d1 Black finishes White off by 4...♛h2+ 5 ♔f1 ♛h1 checkmate.

Instead of castling into the attack, White should aim to put his king on the other side of the board by playing 1 ♗d2, preparing to castle long.

The lesson to be learnt here is to think carefully about the rules. Yes, keep them in mind, but do not follow them slavishly – there will always be exceptions.

Part Two: The Middlegame

Introduction

Assuming that you have followed the first three rules, then you will have brought your pieces into play and your king will be safe at the side of the board. So where do you go from here?

There are two ways of going about trying to win: one can go directly for a checkmating attack against the opponent's king in the middlegame; or, the less direct method, capture enough of the opponent's pieces so that, eventually, he will be powerless to resist an attack against the king.

In modern chess, because both sides usually guard their king well, it is this second method – *material chess* – which is the most common. This leads us directly to the fourth Golden Rule.

Rule 4: Look for captures

When it is your turn to move, always ask yourself: is it possible to capture anything?

Developing a 'good eye' for the board, so that you will quickly recognise the possibilities open to you, is essential if you are to make progress. The necessary skills do not come overnight, but are built over time by practising the game as much as possible. Having said that, even an experienced player will sometimes overlook what is directly under his or her nose.

The following pages contain three sets of six puzzles each. In the first set (pages 46-47), it is possible to capture a piece. Try to find the right move.

The second set of puzzles (pages 50-51) all feature more complex captures. In some of the positions there will be a choice of captures, in others you will have to decide whether it is worth making a capture at all.

In the third set (pages 54-55), you will have to tackle more complex situations. It often happens that one side attacks an enemy unit with several pieces. The defender brings up his reserves to support the threatened unit. Then the question arises as to whether or not the attacker can safely capture the unit which has become the centre of attention. There is actually a simple way to determine whether it is possible to take something when multiple exchanges are involved. *If there is a greater number of attackers than defenders, then generally it is safe to capture.*

Simple tests

In the six positions overleaf, try to find the move which successfully captures an enemy unit.

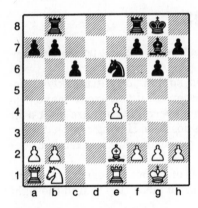

Black to play

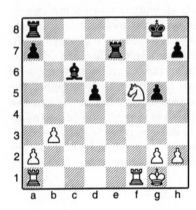

White to play

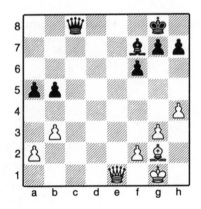

White to play

Black to play

White to play

Black to play

Solutions

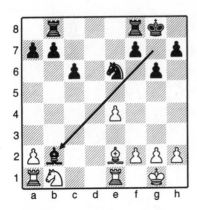

1...♗xb2. The bishop swoops across the board and takes a pawn, with a rook to follow, perhaps?

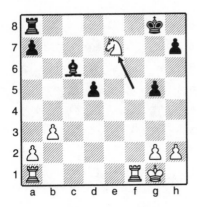

1 ♘xe7+. The knight takes the rook, and at the same time checks the king and attacks a bishop – more on this kind of tactic later.

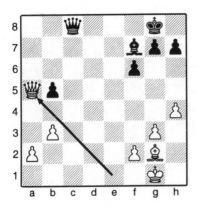

1 ♕xa5. The queen careers off to the left and captures a pawn.

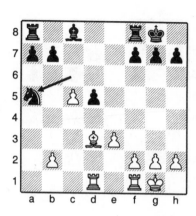

1...♞xa5. The knight captures its opposite number.

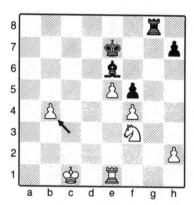

1 cxb4. The pawn captures another pawn.

The rook can take the bishop on c3 or the pawn on h6. Which is best? Have another look at the table on page 21 showing the values of the pieces.

The rook would be recaptured immediately by the king if it took the bishop. As the rook is worth five points and the bishop only three, Black would lose out on this exchange. In view of this it is much better to play more modestly, and just hack off the pawn on h6, so 1...♜xh6 is best.

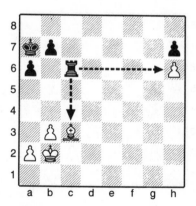

Further practice at capturing

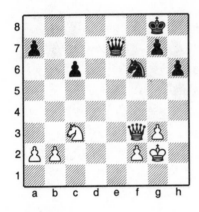

White to play

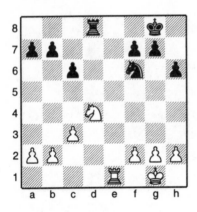

Black to play

White to play

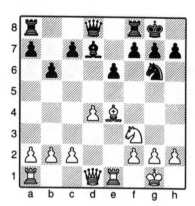

White to play

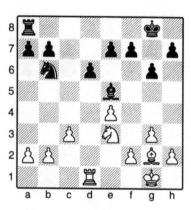

Black to play

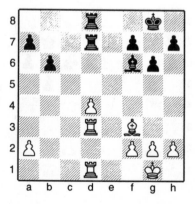

Black to play

Solutions

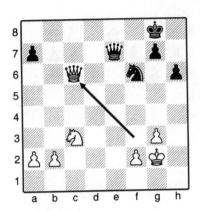

1 ♕xc6. The queen captures the pawn for free. Taking the knight instead would have been disastrous – it was securely protected by a queen and a pawn.

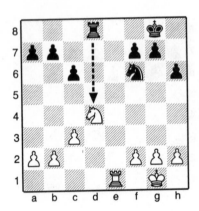

There are no good captures here. It would be a mistake to capture the knight as the rook would be recaptured by the pawn. As the rook is worth five points and the knight only three, Black would lose out.

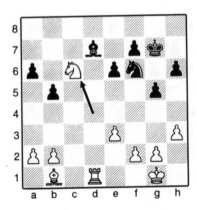

1 ♘xc6. Even though the knight will be taken back immediately, the capture is correct as the rook is worth five points and the knight only three.

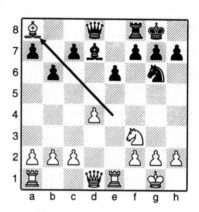

1 ♗xa8. The bishop (worth three points) captures the black rook (worth five points) in the corner – a favourable trade. This was better than taking the knight which is also worth three points.

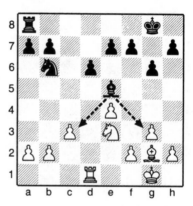

Both of Black's possible captures are poor. There are two pawns which the bishop could possibly capture, but both of them are securely defended by other pawns. Remember, a bishop is worth three points and a pawn just one.

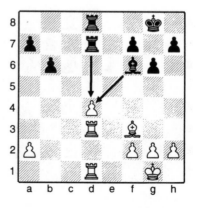

This is the most complicated position. The question is, does Black have enough fire-power to conquer the pawn on d4?

The answer is yes. The pawn can be taken by either bishop or rook, e.g.: 1...♗xd4 2 ♖xd4 ♖xd4 3 ♖xd4 ♖xd4. Black has given up a rook and bishop (a total of eight points) and in return has won a pawn and two rooks (a total of eleven points). After Black took the pawn initially, White should have just cut his losses and left the bishop.

More advanced captures

Examine the following six positions carefully and, using the rule concerning the number of attackers and defenders (see page 45), determine whether it is safe to capture.

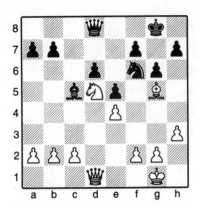

White to play

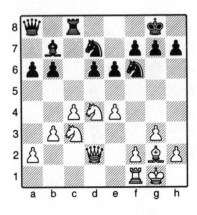

Black to play

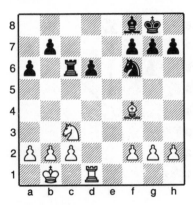

White to play

White to play

Black to play

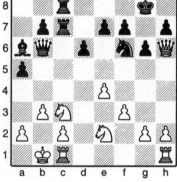

Black to play

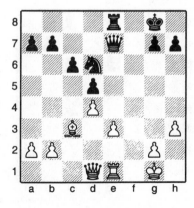

Solutions

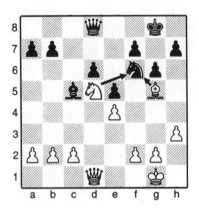

1 ♘xf6+ or 1 ♗xf6. White has two pieces attacking the black knight – the bishop and the knight; and the queen is the only piece defending, so it is safe to capture – with either piece.

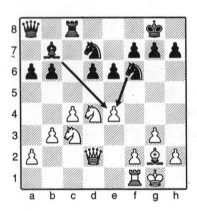

1...♘xe4 or 1...♗xe4. Black has three pieces attacking the e-pawn: the knight, bishop and queen, whereas White has only two defenders. Therefore it is safe to capture.

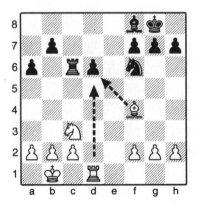

White's bishop and rook are both attacking the d-pawn, but it is adequately defended by Black's bishop and rook. In other words, two attackers versus two defenders, a stand off, so White should not capture the pawn.

1 cxb5 or 1 axb5. White has four
pieces attacking the pawn on b5,
two pawns, a bishop and a rook,
but Black can only muster three
defenders. Therefore it is safe to
take the pawn with either pawn.

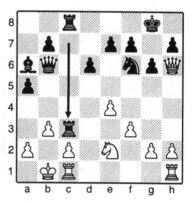

This is more complicated. Let's go
through the options one by one.
  1...♘xe4. A mistake. The knight
can simply be captured by the pawn.
  1...♗xe2. This is not a bad move.
White will take the bishop back
with 2 ♘xe2, then both sides will
have given up a piece worth three
points – an equal exchange.
  1...♖xc3. Best. There are two
men attacking the knight but only
one defending it. After 2 ♘xc3
♖xc3 Black has gained from the
trade: he has taken two knights (2
x 3 points) and only lost a rook (5
points) in return.

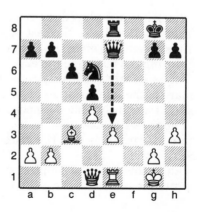

Black has two pieces attacking the
pawn, and White has just one defending, but it would be a mistake
to capture. After 1...♕xe3+ 2 ♖xe3
♖xe3, Black has given up a queen
(nine points) but only gained a rook
and a pawn (six points) in return.
  If Black's pieces were placed the
other way round so that the rook
stood in front of the queen, then it
would be safe to capture.

Rule 5: Study your opponent's last move carefully

How often have I heard the cry from a junior player at a chess club, 'I've got a brilliant plan!' only to find a few moves later that it has all ended in tears: they have become so engrossed in their own ideas that the queen has been swiped from in front of them.

It is easy to forget in the heat of the struggle that one's opponent is also allowed to move, so as well as looking to see whether you can capture any pieces, take care of your own. Always study your opponent's last move carefully – he might be plotting something evil.

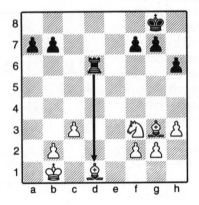

Black has just played the rook to the d-file, threatening to take the bishop on d1. What is the best way of dealing with threat?

It is possible to *move* the bishop in order to save it, for instance, ♗b3 or moving the bishop to the e2, c2 or a4 squares.

Alternatively, the bishop could be *defended* by playing the king one square to the side, to either c1, or c2. The rook is hardly likely to give itself up for a lowly bishop (remember our table of values for the pieces).

The rook's attack could be *blocked* by the knight with 1 ♘d4. Once again, it is unlikely that the more valuable rook will sacrifice itself for the knight.

But in this case, the simplest way of dealing with Black's threat is to *capture* the rook with the bishop: 1 ♗xd6.

Simple tests

Unfortunately it won't always be so easy to counter your opponent's ideas.
In the following positions, ask yourself the purpose of the last move, then decide whether it is best to *move*, *defend*, *block* or *capture*.

Black has just moved the rook across to c8. What is the threat and how would you deal with it?

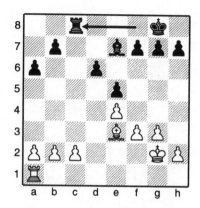

Black has just played the pawn up to a6. What is the threat, and how would you best deal with it?

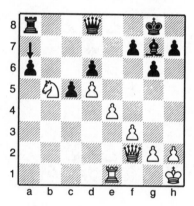

White's queen has retreated from b3 to c2. What is White's threat and how would you deal with it?

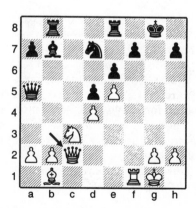

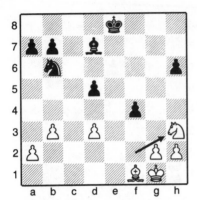

White has just moved the knight from f2 to h3. What is the threat, and how would you deal with it?

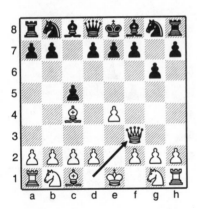

White has just moved the queen out to f3. What is the threat and how would you deal with it?

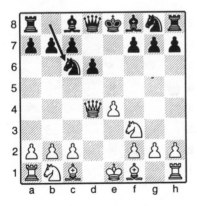

Black has just moved his knight out, at the same time attacking the white queen. The queen could simply move away, but can you see another way of dealing with the threat?

Solutions

1 c3 (or 1 ♖c1). The rook on c8 was attacking the pawn on c2, so the best move for White was to simply move it up one square to where it is *defended* by another pawn. The pawn could also be defended by the white rook, but the pawn advance is to be preferred because it leaves the rook free for more active functions.

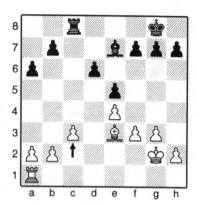

1 ♘a3. The knight was attacked by a pawn so it had to *move*. The a3 square was actually the only safe spot available – check this for yourself.

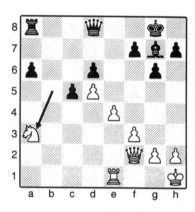

1...♘f8 is best. The white queen and bishop had formed a powerful battery and White was actually threatening to crash down and checkmate the king; however, the knight was able to come to the rescue. By moving to f8, it *defends* the h7 pawn, thus preventing the invasion.

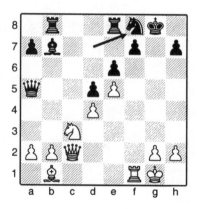

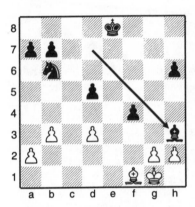

1...♗xh3. The knight on h3 was attacking the pawn on f4. If the pawn moved forward it would have been taken; it couldn't be defended by anything; and, naturally, knight moves cannot be blocked. There was one further option though: the knight could be captured by the bishop. Although the bishop would then be recaptured this would be an equal exchange (bishop and knight are both worth three points).

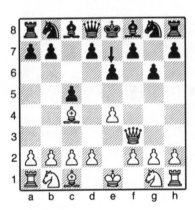

White was threatening one of the oldest tricks in the book, 1 ♕xf7 checkmate (the king cannot capture the queen as it was supported by the bishop). The best method of dealing with this threat is to move the pawn forward to e6, blocking out the white bishop completely. After a few moves it is certain that the white queen will be forced to retreat from its exposed post in the centre as Black's bishops and knight come into play. More on this attempt at a snap checkmate in a later chapter.

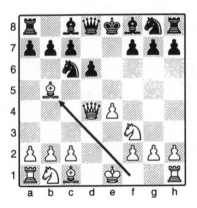

White could have simply moved the attacked queen, but it is better to play 1 ♗b5, which not only meets the attack on the queen, but also develops a piece at the same time. Black cannot take the queen, because this would put his own king in check from the white bishop. This idea is called a *pin*, and we will see more of it in the following section.

Rule 6: Look out for tactics

This is the next step up in our strategy of 'material chess'.

It is not just simple captures that you must learn to be aware of. There are various tricks or 'tactics' that can actually *force* the win of material. This is where the skill lies in a game of chess – to be able to spot these tricks and set them as traps for your opponent.

Among the lethal tactical weapons at your disposal are: the pin; the skewer; the knight fork; destroying the guard; the double attack; trapping; and discovered attacks. You have been warned: chess can be a dirty business.

At first, this myriad of new ideas is all going to seem a little daunting, but don't be put off. I'm not expecting you to remember all these dastardly names and their motifs immediately, just play through them on your board and with a bit of luck your subconscious, at least, will take them in. Then if you practice enough, the patterns will re-appear in your games and begin to look familiar, like words from a long-forgotten language that once more carry meaning.

I would recommend that you play through each tactic in turn on your chessboard to make sure that you understand the idea behind it. The first tactic we shall consider is one which we have encountered already, namely the pin. This motif is highly effective, and crops up in many different situations.

The pin

The pin is an attack against two or more enemy pieces standing in a straight line (be it file, rank, or diagonal). What makes the pin so lethal is that the pinned piece cannot move for fear of exposing the piece behind it.

This sounds complicated in theory, but it's plain when you see it in practice.

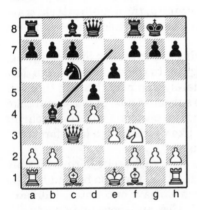

The black bishop has just moved to b4 attacking the white queen, which finds itself unable to move away, for the king would then be in check. We say that the queen is pinned to the king. On the next turn Black will simply be able to capture it, as if White captures the bishop, the black knight takes the queen.

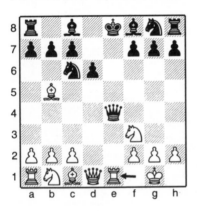

This is similar to some of the positions we saw in the earlier chapters on the opening; do you remember them?

The rook has just moved to e1 pinning the black queen to the king; the queen cannot move away because then the king would be in check, so it is lost.

Pinning a knight against the queen using a bishop is extremely common in the opening.

If the black knight on f6 were to move, then the bishop would snap off the queen, so White just needs to apply a little pressure on the knight to cause extreme embarrassment. In this position White simply plays 1 e5 attacking the knight. It cannot move, so on the next turn White wins a piece with 2 exf6 (or 2 &xf6).

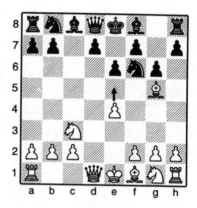

Sometimes a pin can be exploited in the most surprising way.

I vividly remember falling into this trap as a child: I was totally shocked because my position appeared rock solid, and then suddenly ... BLAM!

Black played 1...♕xg3+ smashing into the heart of White's king position, and effectively deciding the game. The queen cannot be taken as the f2 pawn is pinned to the king by the bishop on a7.

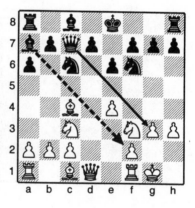

In this position White can set up a pin that will win material. How?

White to play (Solution on page 123.)

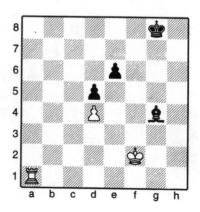

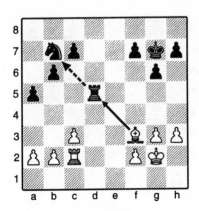

The skewer

The skewer operates by piercing through a piece in order to transfix another on the same straight line. Sounds nasty? You bet.

Here White has just moved the bishop to f3 where it attacks Black's rook; if the rook moves, then the bishop captures the knight.

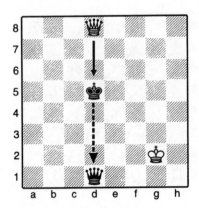

This is another classic example of a skewer. Here Black's king must move out of check, and then the queen is lost.

Clearly, there is a close connection between the pin and the skewer. The difference is that with a skewer, the stronger piece is generally the first one in the line of fire.

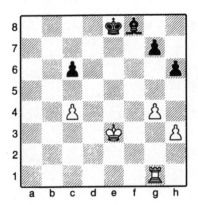

Find the skewer that forces the win of White's rook on g1. (Solution on page 123.)

The knight fork

The knight fork is a deadly and common tactic.

Here, Black has played his knight in to check the king, and at the same time it attacks the rook. White's king must move out of check, but then the knight captures the rook, leaving Black with an overwhelming material advantage.

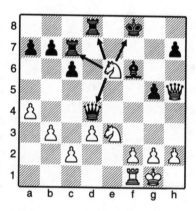

The knight has just moved in to e6, checking the king and attacking all of Black's most important pieces. For obvious reasons this is known as a 'family fork'. Once the king moves White should of course go for the biggest prize: the queen.

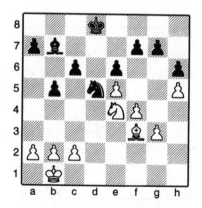

Using a knight fork White (to play) may win a crucial pawn in this position. How? (Solution on page 123.)

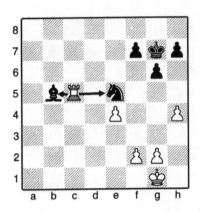

The double attack

This is fairly self-explanatory. With just one move, two threats are simultaneously created, causing extreme embarrassment. Here is a simple example (see top diagram):

White's rook has just moved to the c5 square, attacking both the bishop and the knight; it is impossible for Black to deal with both threats, so he loses a piece by force.

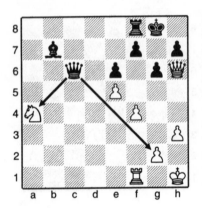

A double attack isn't necessarily directed against two pieces. It could mean that a piece is attacked and at the same time another kind of threat is established. Once again, it all becomes much clearer with a diagram.

The black queen has just moved to c6, setting up a mate threat, together with the bishop, against the g2 pawn; at the same time, the queen attacks the knight on a4. Once again, White is unable to deal with both threats, so must lose a piece.

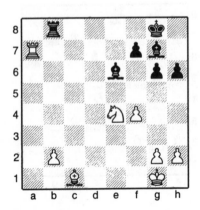

In this position, try to find a double attack that wins White's rook. (Solution on page 123.)

Black to play

Destroying the guard

Sometimes you can remove one of the enemy pieces to make his whole position collapse like a house of cards. Take a look at this diagram.

White can win a piece by 1 ♗xd5 cxd5 2 ♖xe7. This is a relatively simple tactic. If the rook on e1 takes the enemy bishop on e7 immediately, then Black's knight recaptures: not a healthy exchange for White. However, if White first takes the knight, destroying the bishop's guard, then all will be clear for the rook to crash down.

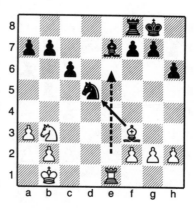

Black has a beautifully centralised knight supported by a bishop on g7, so at the moment 1 ♕xd4 would be unwise because of 1...♗xd4. However if White first plays 1 ♖xg7+, knocking out the bishop. Black recaptures with 1...♔xg7, but then comes 2 ♕xd4+ and White has won a bishop and knight (worth a total of six points) for a rook (worth five points).

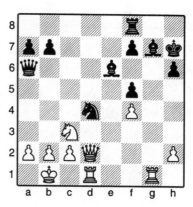

In this position, think carefully about how one might 'destroy the guard' of Black's rook. (Solution on page 123.)

White to play

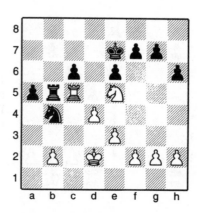

Trapping

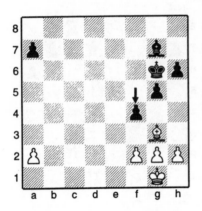

There are many different situations in which a piece can be trapped. Pawns can be useful for this purpose as they are able to advance together creating a tidal wave from which there is no escape.

Black's pawn advances from f5 to f4; White's bishop is attacked and has no safe square that it can escape to.

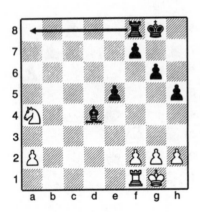

Here, the knight has been trapped at the side of the board by the beautifully centralised bishop on d4 – check all the knight moves for yourself, the bishop has them all covered. All it needs is for the rook to swing across to attack the knight, and Black wins a piece. So 1...♖a8 is the star move.

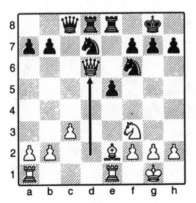

In this position White's queen has lunged forward deep into the heart of Black's territory. Find a good riposte for Black. (Solution on page 123.)

Discovered attacks

Here we reveal a very sneaky idea, whereby a piece moves, threatening, capturing, or checking, and at the same time uncovers an attack on another piece. This is known as a discovered attack.

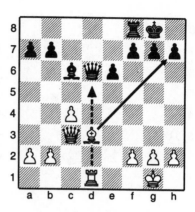

Black's position looks safe and solid, but there is a shock awaiting him. The bishop captures the pawn on h7 *with check*, 1 ♗xh7+, and at the same time unmasks the rook on d1. Black must get out of check by 1...♔xh7 and then the rook takes the queen, 2 ♖xd6. White has won material.

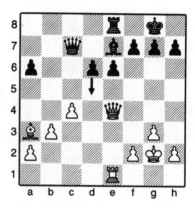

Discovered attacks can appear at the most surprising moments. Here, one small pawn push is enough to win material for Black. After 1...d5 the white queen is attacked and at the same time the diagonal of the bishop on e7 is opened towards the white bishop on a3. Naturally, White must deal with the threat to the queen, the more valuable piece, by 2 cxd5 but then comes 2...♗xa3 and Black has won the bishop.

In this position can you see a way in which White (to play) can use a form of discovered attack to win Black's queen? (Solution on page 123.)

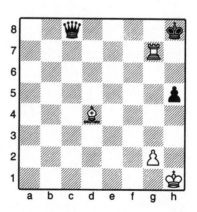

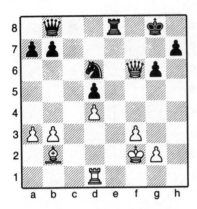

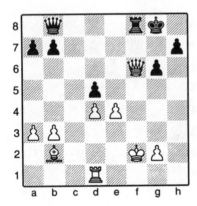

Combined attacks

The tactical themes mentioned here are basic elements; often they are combined to produce more complex tactics. The next position will give you a taste of this.

Black can win White's queen by playing ...

    1   ...   ♘e4+

...forking king and queen. The only way out is to capture the knight by ...

    2   fxe4

...which opens up White's king, allowing

    2   ...   ♖f8

pinning the queen to the king (see bottom diagram).

Exercises

The following positions demonstrate the tactical themes considered above. However, it will not be stated which tactic you are looking for – no one will be standing behind you in a game giving you clues! In each case find the move that wins material. (Solutions on page 123-124.)

Black to play

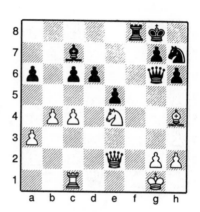

White to play

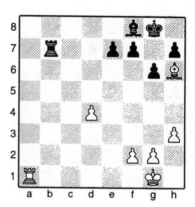

White to play

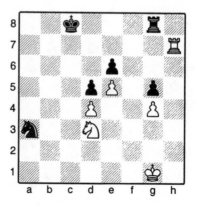

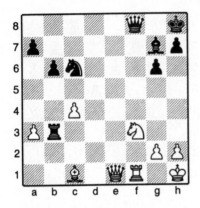

White to play

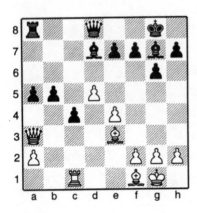

Black to play

Black to play

Black to play

White to play

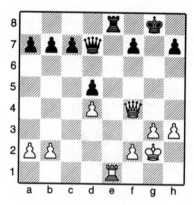

White to play

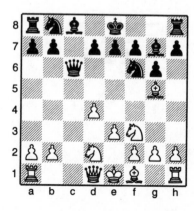

Rule 7: Go for the king

As you will remember, at the start of this section we discussed two ways of playing the middlegame. We have just looked at the first one – material chess – in which you try to win more pieces than your opponent, and then slowly work your way to victory; and now we are going to look at the more direct way of winning: *going for the king*.

If you attack with too few pieces, or in the wrong way, then an attack on the king can be risky as you will just be beaten back. It is important to be able to recognise the situations in which you might succeed with a checkmating attack.

By studying typical checkmating positions you will have a better idea of what you are aiming for, and what the chances are of being successful.

These are all simplified positions showing checkmating patterns around a king that has already castled – that is the most likely place you will find the king if you are playing someone of a decent strength.

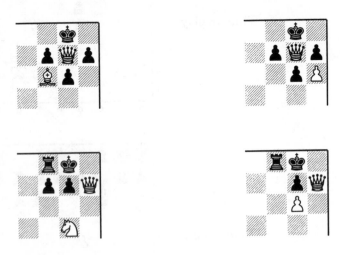

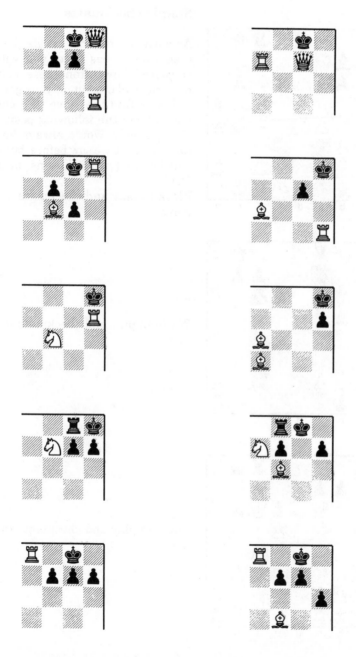

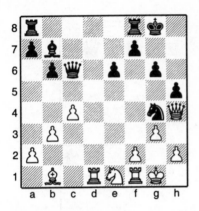

Simple checkmates

As with the tactical motifs, having seen these ideas once, you will be surprised how often these mating patterns will crop up in your games.

Try to find the move that checkmates from the following positions. The patterns won't always be the same as those we saw before, but they will be related. (Solutions on page 124.)

Black to play and checkmate in one move.

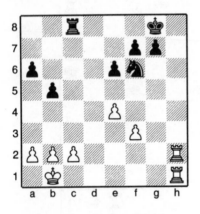

White to play and checkmate in one move.

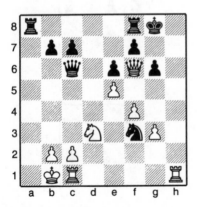

Black to play and checkmate in one move.

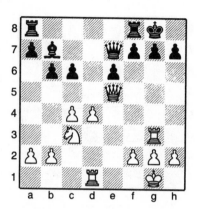

White to play and checkmate in one move.

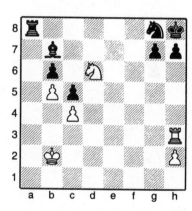

White to play and checkmate in one move.

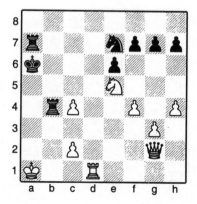

Black to play and checkmate in one move.

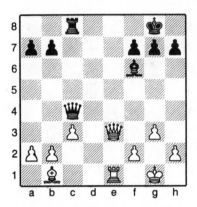

More advanced checkmates

This next set of positions are slightly more difficult: you will have to look more than one move ahead, though hopefully the prototype checkmating positions that we looked at earlier will help you out. (Solutions on page 124.)

White to play and force checkmate in two moves.

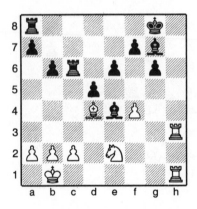

White to play and force checkmate in two moves.

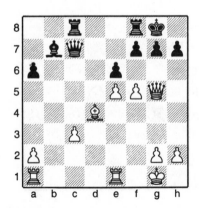

White to play and force checkmate in three moves.

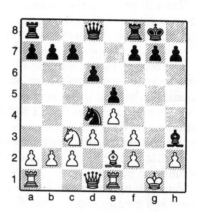

Black to play and force checkmate in two moves.

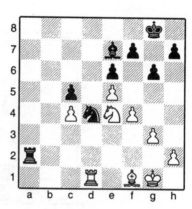

Black to play and force checkmate in two moves.

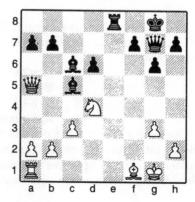

Black to play and force checkmate in two moves.

How to Win at Chess

You will improve the chances of one of these combinations appearing in your games if you create the right conditions. In this next section we will be looking at possible ways of starting an attack.

The best chance of landing a big knock-out punch is if you manage to expose your opponent's king. We have already seen in the first three Golden Rules that if the king gets stuck in the centre of the board, then there is a good chance that it will fall prey to a violent attack as the position opens up. This is one of the points of castling, to bring the king to safety behind a protective barrier of pawns.

So this is the challenge, how are we going to prise the king out from behind the pawns?

Very often, if you can create an open file in front of the king then there is a greater chance that the attack will succeed.

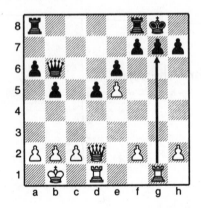

For instance, in this diagram, White's rook stands on the same line as Black's king. True, there is a pawn in the way, but White can blast through with:

1	♖xg7+	♚xg7
2	♕g5+	♚h8
3	♕f6+	♚g8
4	♖g1 checkmate	

Opening a file in front of your opponent's king does not guarantee checkmate, that will depend on many other factors such as: Are there sufficient attacking pieces? Or does your opponent have any counter-play? But it will increase your chances of something 'turning up'.

It is rare, however, that there will be an open file ready for you in front of your opponent's castled king; usually you will have to work to create one.

If you have castled on the opposite side to your opponent, i.e. one player has castled queenside and the other on the kingside, then a familiar method of opening a file is to use the pawns either as a battering ram, or simply as the advance rider in front of a rook – as in the next example.

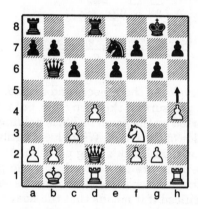

White has every chance of succeeding with his attack if he plays:

1 h5

cracking open the h-file.

There is little that Black can do to prevent White from playing on the next turn 2 hxg6, and the rook on h1, combined with the white queen coming in to h6, should prove decisive.

This next position is more complicated, but demonstrates exactly the same strategy: opening files for the rooks in front of the king. It comes from the concluding phase of a game played between two of Hungary's leading players in 1979.

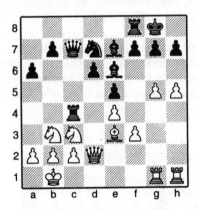

Both sides have developed their pieces and castled. Black is attempting to build up some pressure on the open c-file, but for the moment the knight on c3, supported by the pawn on b2, is holding the fort successfully. On the other side of the board, White has craftily placed his rooks so that they bear down on Black's king position. At the moment, the files in front of the king are still closed, but the pawns have been thrown forward as the first wave of attack: they are less valuable pieces so a few can be sacrificed if it means that the heavier men get a good shot at the king.

1   g6

This guarantees that at least one file will be opened for the rooks. Let's look at some of Black's options:

1...fxg6 2 hxg6 hxg6 3 ♖xg6, and White is ready to pile up the rooks against the pawn in front of Black's king;

If Black tries to keep the position closed with 1...h6, then comes a bishop sacrifice to smash through the defences: 2 ♗xh6 gxh6 3 ♕xh6 and mate follows shortly.

Instead, in the game itself Black chose to ignore everything, but unfortunately for him, the attack did not go away. (Incidentally, if White had erroneously played the other pawn forward with 1 h6, it would have given Black the opportunity to close the position in front of his king with 1...g6.)

1   ...   ♖c8

2   ♗h6

A stunner. White could open the file straight away, but throws the bishop on the fire to make sure that Black's king really gets hammered.

If the piece is taken, 2...gxh6, then the entry of the queen into the game with 3 ♕xh6 will quickly decide the issue.

The queen is a deadly attacking unit, but it needs to work in concert with the other pieces. Note how in this game it only enters the attack after a safe way through has been cleared by the pawns and the bishop.

2	...	♗f6
3	gxh7+	♔xh7

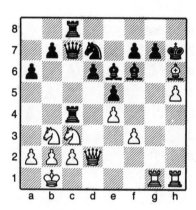

4	♗xg7

Often it can be worth giving up a piece in order to lay bare the king.

4	...	♗xg7
5	h6	

Threatening the bishop and forcing it to move.

5	...	♗f6
6	♕g2	

...and here Black actually resigned! The threat is 7 ♕g7+, Black must of course capture, 7...♗xg7, and then comes 8 hxg7+ ♔g8 9 ♖h8 checkmate. Black has no method of parrying the attack.

When kings castle on opposite wings, launching an attack with pawns is, as we have seen, not out of the question. However, if the kings have castled on the same side, then attacking with pawns can be suicidal: unless you have a very good reason, you should never move the pawns up in front of your own king. If you think back you will recall that the whole idea behind castling was that the pawns could offer the king decent protection.

Launching an attack without the aid of pawns to open lines is more difficult, though not impossible: often a piece will have to be sacrificed in order to expose the king. Bringing a rook into the attack in combination with the queen is, as we have seen, the most effective method of attacking, but this becomes more problematic when the rook has to move up and across the board – there is more chance of the manoeuvre being disrupted. But if you think it's possible, then go for it.

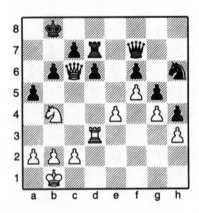

Often the rook is swung up to the third rank (see diagram above) and then across in front of the king. White actually has a winning combination here that shows the rook's potential in such situations:

    1   ♘a6+
If Black now plays 1...♚c8 then 2 ♕a8 is mate, therefore ...

    1   ...   ♚a7
...but now White finds a brilliant way of bringing the rook into the game:

    2   ♘c5
If 2...dxc5, then 3 ♖xd7, so Black tries ...

    2   ...   bxc5
...which allows the rook into the attack along the third rank:

    3   ♖a3
...after which there is nothing to prevent 4 ♖xa5+ ♚b8 5 ♖a8 checkmate.

To finish this chapter, here is an extract from a game showing a quick attack on a castled king and featuring the 'swinging rook' manoeuvre, demonstrated above, though in a slightly different situation. We join the game at White's fourteenth move.

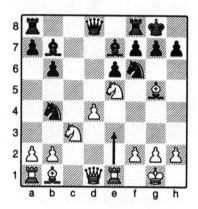

R. Keene – A. Miles
Hastings 1976

Both sides have brought out their pieces and castled. White has a pawn in the centre and a knight positioned on a great square on e5, but Black's position seems safe enough; however, White sees a chance to launch an attack with ...

14 ♖e3

The rook prepares to swing across the board towards the king. The immediate threat is 15 ♗xf6 ♗xf6 16 ♗xh7+ ♔xh7 17 ♕h5+ ♔g8 18 ♖h3, forcing checkmate on h8 or h7.

Unfortunately, Black sees through that one.

14 ... g6

Closing the diagonal of the bishop on b1.

15 ♖g3

The rook is not to be denied; it lines up menacingly, opposite the black king.

15 ... ♖c8

16 ♗h6

The bishop now crowds in next to the king.

16 ... ♖e8

The rook was attacked so it had to move.

17 a3 ♘c6

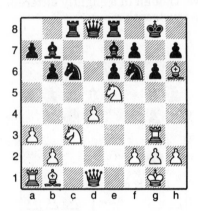

18   ♘xg6

White judges that he can afford to sacrifice two pieces in order to blow open Black's king. This is, of course, extremely risky, for if the attack fails then White will be left with, technically, a lost position as he has given away so much material.

18   ...   hxg6
19   ♗xg6

Another piece is given up for the cause, but White is whittling away the Black king's defensive pawn shield.

19   ...   fxg6

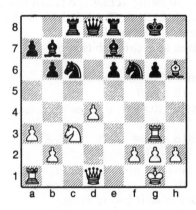

This next move is the most difficult of the whole game. Instead of continuing the attack solely with the rook, White realises that his queen needs to enter the game. There are a number of squares available to the queen that look plausible, but only one will do.

        20 ♕b1

It looks crazy to put the queen so far out to the side of the board, but it is about to rebound into the heart of the attack.

If instead 20 ♕d3, Black had a clever defence: 20...♘e5 – defending the g-pawn – and if 21 dxe5 ♕xd3 22 ♖xd3 ♘d5, Black has managed to exchange queens, the attack is over, and he remains with an extra piece.

If 20 ♕c2, then once again 20...♘e5 21 dxe5 ♘e4 – exploiting a pin to block the path of the queen: 22 ♘xe4 is impossible because of 22...♖xc2.

In the game Black thrashes on for a few more moves, but ultimately it is impossible to prevent mate.

        20 ...   ♘e5
        21 dxe5   ♘e4
        22 ♘xe4   ♔h7

.Defending the g-pawn for a moment, but White still crashes through:

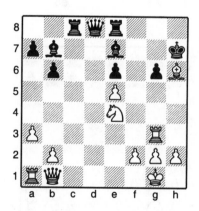

        23 ♘f6+   ♗xf6
        24 ♕xg6+

    The queen finally enters the attack and the effect is immediately decisive.

        24 ...   ♔h8
        25 ♗g7+   ♗xg7
        26 ♕xg7 checkmate

A blistering attack; White's finishing was brutal. Be warned though, this was all finely calculated, if the attack had failed, then Black would have been left with an overwhelming material advantage.

Only begin an attack if you feel you have enough pieces around the king to carry it through, otherwise stick to the strategy of 'material chess'.

Scholar's mate

Before leaving this chapter, it is worth mentioning a dastardly strategy that you might occasionally encounter at the start of the game if you happen to be facing a mean and unscrupulous opponent.

Scholar's mate is an attempt to give checkmate after just four moves from the start of the game. Such an early sortie on the king is not justified; remember, before you launch an attack you should ensure that the conditions are right, i.e. that you have a sufficient number of pieces in place. However, it is worth looking at briefly just so that you know exactly how to deal with it if the occasion should arise.

1   e4   e5

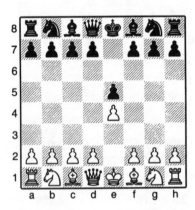

Both sides bring out their pawns in classical fashion.

2   ♗c4   ♗c5

These moves are also fine, if a little boring! If I were Black, I would prefer not to keep everything so symmetrical.

        3   ♕h5

It is this move which is outrageous. If Black is now careless and just thinks about the attack on the e-pawn, defending it with...

        3   ...   ♘c6

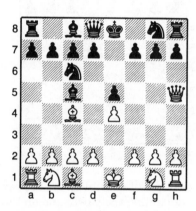

Then the unthinkable happens:

        4 ♕xf7 checkmate

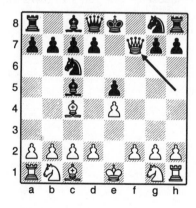

The queen is supported by the bishop and thus cannot be taken.

Let's return to the position after White's queen comes out to h5.

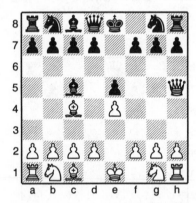

In fact Black has a couple of sensible ways to prevent the mate. The best must be 3...♕e7, defending the pawn, and on the next turn 4...♘f6, attacking the queen which must then retreat, and valuable time has been lost. (Note that 3...g6, blocking the queen's route to f7, would be a mistake due to 4 ♕xe5+ followed by 5 ♕xh8. Ouch!)

Black has created no weaknesses in his position, so such an early attack is never likely to succeed – but you still have to play carefully.

Part Three: The Endgame

Introduction

What happens if, by sheer luck, your opponent manages to survive your onslaught in the middlegame, and struggles on into the endgame? This last section will show you how to play when there are just a few pieces left on the board.

Rule 8: Know the basic checkmates

Supposing you reach the final phase of the game with a material advantage, what should you be aiming for? You can't win a game on points. Checkmate is still the goal, and in order to finish off your opponent at the end of the game, it is essential to know about the basic checkmates. We will begin with the simplest, but perhaps the most important basic endgame, king and queen against king.

King and queen against king

The most important thing to appreciate is that although the queen is the most powerful piece on the board, *it cannot deliver checkmate on its own. It must have the support of the king.*

This can be seen from the two basic checkmating positions of this endgame.

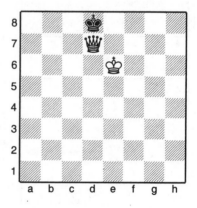

In the first position, the queen has given checkmate on the d7 square: the king is in check and has no place to move to; the queen cannot be taken as it is supported by its own king. Remember, it is illegal for the two kings to stand on adjacent squares.

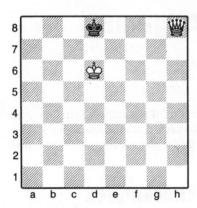

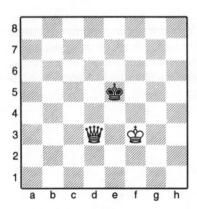

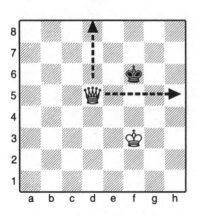

The next position shows the queen checkmating from the side of the board. The black king cannot move up the board because all the squares are covered by White's king.

The other important point to be drawn from these positions is that it is only possible to checkmate the enemy king at the side of the board, so your first task must be to drive it there. The following sequence of moves shows how it is possible to force the opponent's king to the edge (middle diagram):

1   ♕c4

The secret of driving the enemy king back is to restrict its movement, and only to give check when you are certain that it forces a retreat.

1   ...   ♚f5
2   ♕d5+

Because of where the white king stands, the black king is forced backwards after this check.

2   ...   ♚f6

The bottom diagram shows the current situation.

Notice how the queen creates a box, preventing the king from escaping, and thus giving White all the time he needs to bring his own king into play.

3   ♔f4   ♚e7
4   ♕c6

Once again the queen restricts the movement of the king. The king cannot cross the line of the sixth rank because it would be in check.

4   ...   ♚f7

5 ⚔f5

Don't leave the king behind.

5 ... ⚔e7

The diagram on the right shows the present position.

6 ♕c7+

White seizes the chance to force the king onto the back rank; now mate is not far off.

6 ... ⚔f8

7 ⚔f6 ⚔g8

8 ♕g7 checkmate

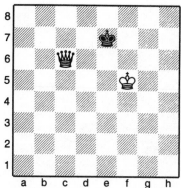

Notice how checks were only given when they fulfilled a specific purpose, in this case driving the king backwards. We all feel good when giving check, because it forces our opponents to deal with the attack to their king before going about their plans; as one old master put it, 'When I give check I fear no one!' But checking alone cannot win a game, it is only a means to an end. Think carefully before you give check, particularly in these simpler endings when it may well be more valuable to restrict your opponent's king before attacking it.

One can of course take this to extremes. There is one trap you should be aware of when playing this ending: stalemate.

If the king is in the corner, then be wary of bringing the queen in too close. With the queen on c7, the black king has no legal moves as it cannot put itself in check. However, it is not actually in check, so the position is stalemate: the game is a draw.

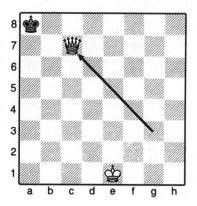

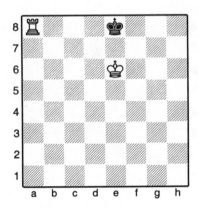

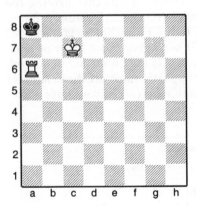

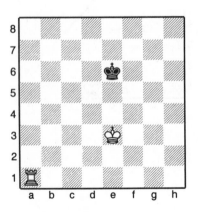

King and rook against king

At first attempt, this seems considerably more difficult than checkmating with the queen, but in fact, the technique is rather similar: restrict your opponent's king using king and rook as a team.

First, let us take a look at the two basic checkmating positions – then you know what to aim for.

The top diagram is almost exactly the same as one of the basic checkmates with the queen. The rook gives checkmate from the side; the black king cannot escape by moving up the board, as the white king guards all the squares.

The other checkmate possible is in the corner of the board. Once again, the king must assist.

Just as when checkmating with the king and queen against king, it is necessary to drive the king to the side of the board. Let's examine how that is best achieved (bottom diagram).

The correct technique is to restrict the mobility of Black's king.

    1   ♜a5

After this move, Black's king may not cross the line of the rook along the fifth rank.

    1 ...   ♔d6
    2 ♔d4

It is essential to bring the king up to support the rook.

    2 ...   ♔c6

3 ♖d5

This is the best move in the position (see top diagram on right). Instead of checking the king, the rook is used to restrict its movement. Black's king is now confined within the box created by the rook.

3 ... ♚b6

4 ♖c5

The box confining Black's king grows smaller.

4 ... ♚b7

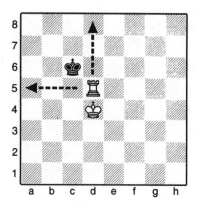

5 ♔d5

(See middle diagram.)

It is impossible to restrict Black's king further with the rook, so the king is brought closer.

5 ... ♚b6

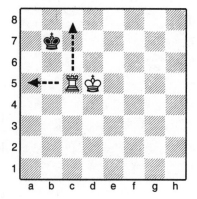

6 ♔d6

(See bottom diagram.)

Again, it was not possible to improve the position of the rook, so the king is brought forward. Black's king is forced to retreat as it is still confined within the box created by the rook.

6 ... ♚b7

7 ♖c6

The box confining the king gradually grows smaller.

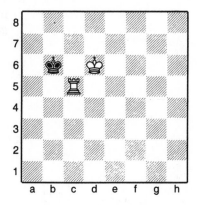

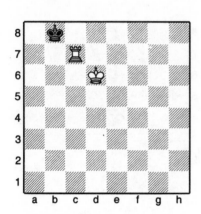

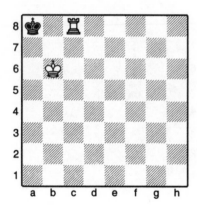

7 ...   ♚b8
8 ♖c7
(See top diagram.)

The king is now trapped on the back rank and, so long as the rook remains in place, may only shuffle back and forth between two squares.

8 ...   ♚a8

9 ♔c6   ♚b8
10 ♔b6   ♚a8
11 ♖c8 checkmate

Notice how in the process of driving Black's king into the corner, it was more important to restrict the king than to check it.

It is best to practice these basic checkmating ideas with a partner. Understanding the necessary techniques will enormously improve your game.

Two rooks against a king

Checkmating with two rooks is much the easiest to learn of the basic endings – perhaps I shouldn't have left it until last!

When checkmating with a lone queen or rook, the basic idea is to restrict the movement of the king; it is the same case here (top diagram).

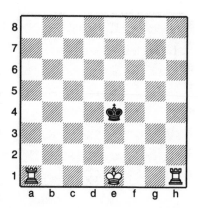

1 Rh3

Black's king may not cross the line of White's rook: the confining begins.

1 ... Kf4

2 Ra4+

The king is in check and must move backwards.

2 ... Kf5

3 Rh5+

Once again forcing the king back.

3 ... Kg6

4 Rb5

(See middle diagram.)

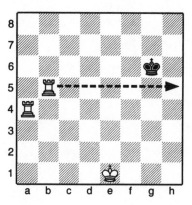

The best move. Rooks are long-range pieces and therefore operate best when they are as far away from the enemy king as possible. From a distance they command just as many squares as close up, but cannot be hassled by the king.

The king cannot cross the line of the rook while it stands on the fifth rank.

4 ... Kf6

5 Ra6+

(See bottom diagram.)

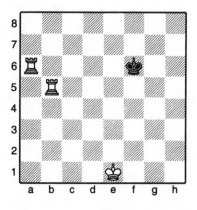

While one rook restricts the king, the other checks it, forcing it backwards.

5 ... Ke7

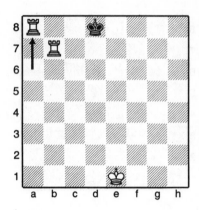

Black's king is forced to retreat: it cannot cross the line of the rook.

6   ♖b7+   ♚d8

7   ♖a8 checkmate

The rooks work as a great team, rolling down the board together. In the checkmating position itself, one of them deals the final deadly blow while the other prevents the king moving away.

Unlike checkmating with a lone queen or rook, checkmating with two rooks does not require the participation of the king – assuming you have mastered the technique above.

Rule 9: Make a new queen

If you are playing against someone of similar strength, you could find yourself in an endgame in which both sides have roughly the same number of pieces on the board. In that case it will not be possible to go for one of the basic checkmates straightaway as discussed in the last rule. First it will be necessary to make a new queen. This can be done by forcing a pawn through to the eighth rank and promoting it into a queen (it is also possible to get a rook, or a bishop, or a knight, but as the queen is the most powerful piece, this is almost always the best choice).

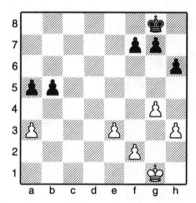

Black is able to win this position very easily by simply pushing a pawn down to the eighth rank to get a queen:

1	...	b4
2	axb4	axb4
3	♔f1	

The king runs over to try to stop the pawn, but does not make it in time.

3	...	b3
4	♔e1	b2
5	♔d2	b1♕

Black makes a queen and will be able to win easily by gradually liquidating the remaining pawns, and then bringing up the king to assist with checkmating.

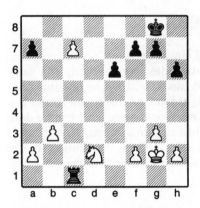

Take a look at these more complex positions; see if you can find the right move to force a pawn through to the queening square.

White to play

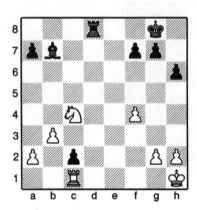

Black to play

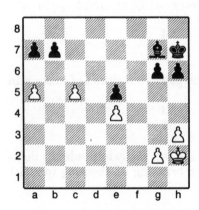

White to play

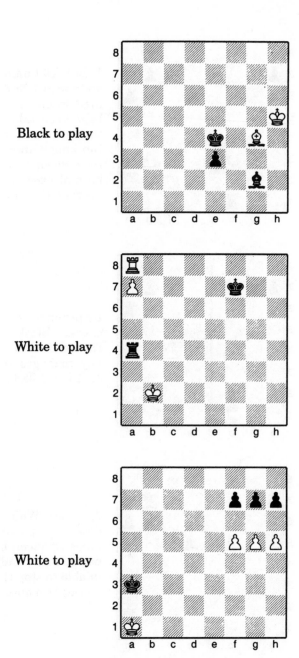

Black to play

White to play

White to play

How to Win at Chess

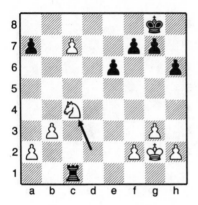

1 ♘c4. Obtaining a queen immediately with 1 c8♕+ was possible, but inadvisable: the new queen would have been taken off right away by the rook on c1. However, by playing the knight into c4, the path of the rook down towards the pawn has been blocked, and Black is unable to prevent the pawn queening on the next turn.

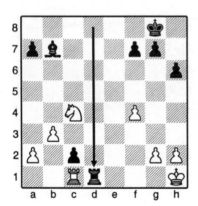

By playing the rook down to d1 with check, Black forces the pawn through, and at the same time actually manages to force checkmate: 1...♖d1+ 2 ♖xd1 cxd1♕ checkmate.

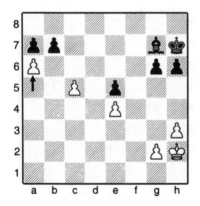

Although White is a whole bishop down it is possible to force a pawn home to queen by sacrificing the a-pawn: 1 a6 bxa6 2 c6, and Black is unable to stop the c-pawn from promoting to a queen.

The easiest way of forcing the pawn through to the queening square is by blocking out the enemy bishop with 1...♝f3; if White exchanges, 2 ♗xf3+ ♚xf3, then the e-pawn has a clear run to e1, after which an ending of queen and king against king results, which, as we have already seen, it is possible to win.

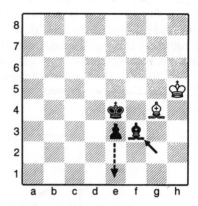

Although White's pawn is just one square from queening, there is only one way to win this position, and that is by the sneaky rook move 1 ♖h8, as shown in the diagram. Now there is a threat to queen the pawn, so Black plays 1...♖xa7 – it seems as though he has escaped; wrong. A fiendish skewer has been set up: 2 ♖h7+ ♚g6 3 ♖xa7, and White has reached the winning ending of king and rook against king.

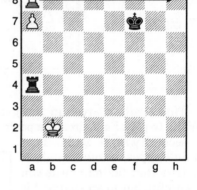

If you got this one, well done, it is extremely tricky. I am giving it here more to show the possibilities of a dynamic breakthrough in the ending than anything else (sorry if you were baffled). White can force a pawn through by sacrificing two pawns, beginning with:

1 g6
If 1...fxg6 2 h6 gxh6 3 f6, and the f-pawn queens; or if 1...hxg6 2 f6 gxf6 3 h6, and the white h-pawn queens.

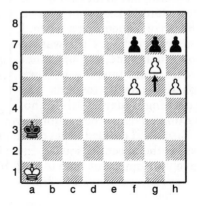

In all of these positions, one side or the other had a pawn on the verge of queening; it is important to realise that they did not get there by accident. In an ending, if you have a pawn that has a clear path through to the eighth rank, you should push it. If nothing else, it will distract your opponent from his own plans.

Just to show that I practice what I preach, take a look at this position from one of my own games:

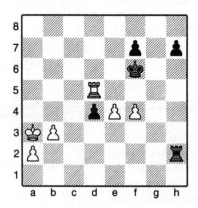

This position arose in the game King-Webb, London 1994, with White to play. I am already a pawn up, and I have the possibility to take a second with 1 ♖xd4. That didn't appeal to me though. It is true that taking pawns can be useful, but in an ending it is important to keep your eyes on the prize – queening a pawn. I was worried that if I wasted too much time, my opponent would start pushing his own 'passed pawn' towards the queening square with 1...h5, setting up dangerous counterplay.

> **What's a Passed Pawn?**
>
> A 'passed pawn' is one which has no other pawns blocking or impeding its path towards the eighth rank. Thus in the above diagram there are actually four passed pawns: White's a- and b-pawns, and Black's d- and h-pawns.

Instead, I decided to get one of my own passed pawns rolling towards the queening square. In endings, activity is the key word – don't give your opponent time to push his own pawns.

1   b4

Although still quite a few squares from the eighth rank, the pawn already poses a problem for Black as his king is unable to march across and block it, owing to the beautifully centralised position of White's rook.

1	...	♖f2

Black attacks a pawn, but is this relevant? I am not going to be distracted from the task: push the pawn.

2	b5	♖xf4
3	♖xd4	

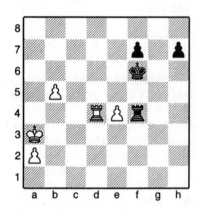

Now I felt that it was appropriate to take this pawn, as I can do so with gain of time: Black does not have time to push his own pawn with 3...h5 as I can simplify with 4 e5+ ♔xe5 5 ♖xf4 ♔xf4 6 b6, when the pawn cannot be prevented from marching to the queening square.

3	...	♔e5

Preventing the trick, but giving me the opportunity to redeploy my rook to an excellent square.

4	♖b4

With the rook behind it, the pawn gains even more muscle. Black's rook must retreat in order to block it.

4	...	♖g4
5	b6	♖g8
6	b7	♖b8

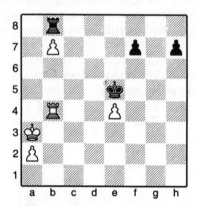

Now that the rook is reduced to complete passivity, White's task is relatively simple. It is time to bring in the king – see Rule 10!

    7   ♖a4

The threat is clear: to march the king up to attack Black's rook. Black tries to bring his own king across to defend, but with the rook so passive it is all in vain.

    7   ...   ♚d6
    8   ♖a5   ♚c5
    9   ♜b1

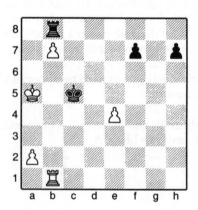

As I mentioned before in one of the earlier rules on the endgame, rooks are long-range pieces; in general they work at their best far away from the enemy king where they are still just as powerful, but cannot be hassled. This is exactly the case here.

Black chose to resign here as he could find no defence to White's king march. If 9...♚c6, 10 ♚a6 followed by 11 ♖c1+, driving Black's king away, and 12 ♚a7, forcing the win of Black's rook for the pawn.

This last example brings us neatly on to Rule 10 ...

Rule 10: Use your king

In the opening and middlegame, it is vital that your king remains well protected. As we have seen, if it becomes exposed then it might be gunned down.

However, in the endgame, when there are fewer pieces left on the board, the situation changes: the king can often be one of your best attacking pieces.

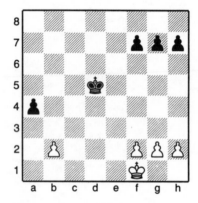

Both sides have the same number of pieces, but it is Black who stands well because his king is so actively placed. In fact, he wins very easily by playing the king forward to take the b-pawn:

1	...	♚c4
2	♔e2	♚b3
3	♔d2	♚xb2
4	♔d3	a3

...and nothing can prevent the pawn from plodding down to become a queen. If White's king had been further towards the left at the beginning, ready to block out the king, then he would have been able to hold the pawn and save the game.

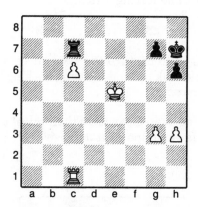

This is another simple, yet common, example of how an active king can decide the game. The black rook is preventing the pawn on c6 from moving down the board, but the blockade can be broken with ease by White's king:

      1   ♔d6

The rook is attacked and must retreat.

      1   ...   ♖c8

The pawn can now advance one square closer to the eighth rank.

      2   c7   ♔g6

The king moves over, but it is too late.

      3   ♔d7

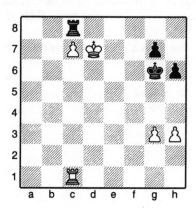

Attacking the rook and forcing it to move.

3	...	♖f8
4	c8♕	♖xc8
5	♖xc8	

Black has managed to capture the new queen with his rook, but White is now a whole rook up, and by using his king and rook to attack together, he will win easily.

As well as assisting passed pawns in their quest to become a queen, the king can also play an important defensive role by moving into the centre of the board.

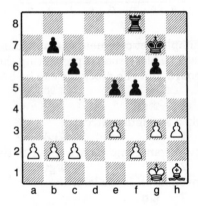

In this position Black is threatening to devastate the pawns on the queenside by playing ...♖d8, followed by ...♖d2 and ♖xc2, ♖xb2 and ♖xa2. Deadly.

However, White is able to prevent this idea by moving his king towards the centre of the board.

1	♔f1	♖d8
2	♔e2	

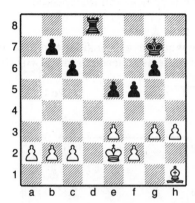

The rook's invasion has been prevented, and chances are roughly balanced.

Here is one final example of the power of the king by one of the greatest endgame experts in the world, Viktor Korchnoi.

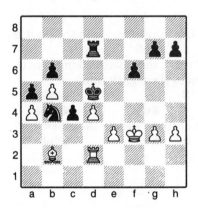

This position is from the game Bischoff-Korchnoi, Lugano 1982.

Black's king is in the centre of the board, and he has a strong passed pawn on c4. However, it is not easy to see how to make progress from here. If 1...♖c7, threatening to push the pawn, then 2 e4+, driving the king back, 2...♔d6, and then the c-pawn can be blockaded with 3 ♗c3.

Korchnoi's solution is radical and unexpected.

1	...	c3
2	♗xc3	

How many people would even consider the idea of giving up one of their strongest assets, the advanced passed pawn? Korchnoi has found a brilliant plan.

2	...	♔c4

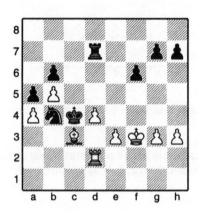

This is the point, the king enters into the position.

3	♗b2	

If instead 3 ♗xb4 axb4, then Black's king is in the perfect position to shepherd the b-pawn to the eighth rank.

3	...	♔b3
4	♔e2	♔xa4

This was the goal of Black's king, the a-pawn.

5	♗c3	♔b3

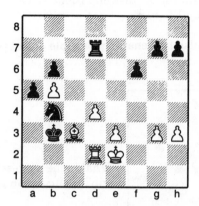

Brilliant. Instead of taking the b-pawn, the king maintains its position deep in the heart of White's camp, preparing to support the a-pawn in its march to the queening square.

   6 ♗xb4

If instead 6 ♗b2, then 6...a4, and White will be forced to give up the bishop for the pawn.

   6 ...   axb4

Black's king is in the perfect position to support the b-pawn.

   7 ♔d3   ♔a3
   8 ♖c2   b3
   9 ♖c8   ♖a7

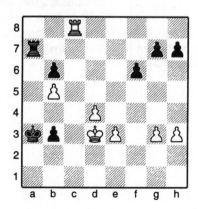

...and there is nothing to prevent Black from playing 10...b2 and 11...♚a2, followed by 12...b1♛.

And finally, to finish this chapter, a couple of test positions.

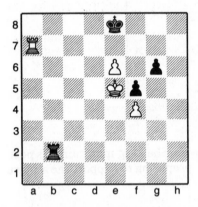

What is the simplest way for White to win? (Solution on page 125.)

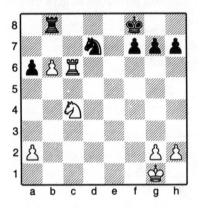

White has a far advanced passed pawn on b6, but for the moment its progress towards the queening square has been blocked by Black's rook. Think of a good plan for White that might help in getting the pawn moving again. (Solution on page 125.)

Exercises

The last section of the book contains a selection of positions for the reader to tackle. It is possible to solve all these positions using the ideas explained in this book, although in some cases a little imagination is necessary as well. There are no hints as to which idea belongs with which position.

White to play can take a pawn by 1 ♖xh6. Is this a good move?

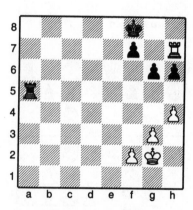

Black to move

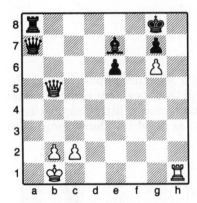

Black is threatening instant checkmate by ...♛a1, but it is White's turn to move. What should he play?

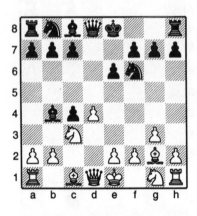

White to play

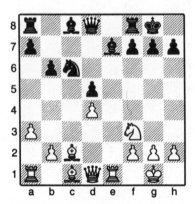

How can White, to play, win a pawn?

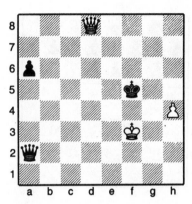

White to play

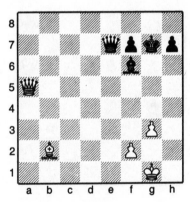

White to play

Black has just given check by playing his rook to c1. What is White's best method of meeting the check?

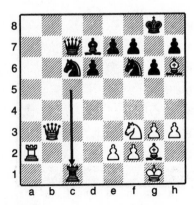

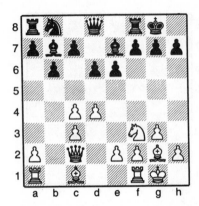

White to play

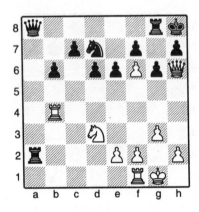

White to play

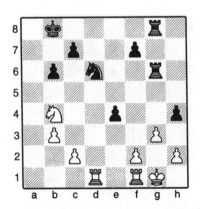

White to play

White to play

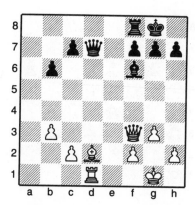

White to play

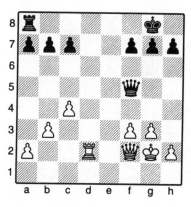

White to play

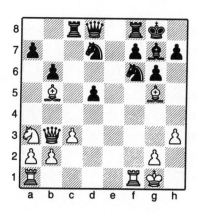

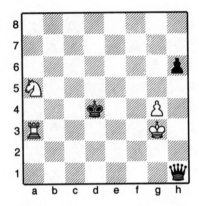

White to play

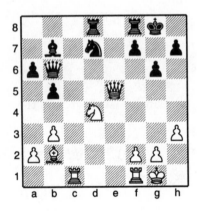

White to play

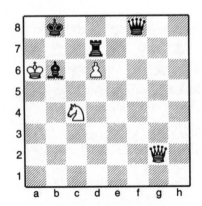

White to play

Solutions

Page 9 (understanding notation): The marked squares are: a2, c4, d7, g6, h3.

Page 13 (introduction): 1 ♕c4.

Page 29: (Rule 3) 1 ♖e1.

Page 65 (bottom diagram): 1 ♖g1. The bishop cannot escape.

Page 66 (bottom diagram): 1...♗c5+. The king must move, and then Black takes the rook on g1.

Page 67 (bottom diagram): 1 ♘d6. White attacks the bishop and the pawn on f7.

Page 68 (bottom diagram): 1...♗d4+. The king must move, and then Black takes the rook on a7.

Page 69 (bottom diagram): After 1 ♘xc6+ ♘xc6 2 ♖xb5 White has won a rook and a pawn (six points) in return for a knight (three points).

Page 70 (bottom diagram): 1...♘c5. White's queen is attacked by the rook on d8, and is unable to escape.

Page 71 (bottom diagram): 1 ♖c7+. The rook uncovers a check from the bishop on d4 (a 'discovered check'); the black king must move, and then comes 2 ♖xc8+.

Page 73 (top diagram): This is an example of a double attack. 1...♖f4 attacks both bishop and knight so forces the win of a piece.

Page 73 (middle diagram): 1 ♖a8. White pins the bishop on f8 and, incidentally, sets up an unstoppable mate threat, 2 ♖xf8.

Page 73 (bottom diagram): 1 ♖a7. The rook attacks the knight on a3, and at the same time threatens 2 ♖a8+ winning the rook on g8.

Page 74 (top diagram): 1 ♘d2. An unexpected discovered attack. The knight attacks the rook on b3, and at the same time unmasks an attack of the rook on f1 to the black queen.

Page 74 (middle diagram): 1...b4. The queen is trapped.

Page 74 (bottom diagram): 1...♘c7. The knight forks queen and rook.

Page 75 (top diagram): 1...♗e6. Skewering queen and rook.

Page 75 (middle diagram): 1 ♕g4+ – destroying the guard of the rook on e8 – 1...♕xg4 2 ♖xe8+ ♔g7 3 hxg4.

Page 75 (bottom diagram): 1 ♖c1. The queen is skewered to the bishop; if the queen moves then 2 ♖xc8 is mate.

Page 78 (top diagram): 1...♕h1 mate.

Page 78 (middle diagram): 1 ♖h8 mate.

Page 78 (bottom diagram): 1...♘d2 mate.

Page 79 (top diagram): 1 ♕xg7 mate.

Page 79 (middle diagram): 1 ♘f7 mate.

Page 79 (bottom diagram): 1...♔b6 mate.

Page 80 (top diagram): 1 ♕e8+ ♖xe8 2 ♖xe8 mate.

Page 80 (middle diagram): 1 ♖h8+ ♗xh8 2 ♖xh8 mate.

Page 80 (bottom diagram): 1 f6 g6 2 ♕h6 and 3 ♕g7 mate.

Page 81 (top diagram): 1...♕g5+ 2 ♔h1 ♕g2 mate.

Page 81 (middle diagram): 1...♘f3+ 2 ♔h1 ♖xh2 mate.

Page 81 (bottom diagram): 1...♗xd4+ 2 cxd4 ♕xd4 mate or 1...♕xd4+ 2 cxd4 ♗xd4 mate.

Page 116 (top diagram): The strongest move is 1 ♘f6, threatening 2 ♖a8 mate. If 1...♖b8, then 2 ♖h7 ♔d8 3 ♖h8+ ♔c7 4 ♖xb8 ♔xb8 5 e7 wins for White.

Page 116 (bottom diagram): (King – Grün, Germany 1986) After 1 ♔f2 the plan is simple: to march the king over to take the a-pawn, ♔e3-d4-c3-b4-a5 xa6. There is little that Black can do to prevent it. The game concluded 1...♔e7 2 ♔e3 a5 3 ♔d4 a4 4 ♔c3 f6 5 ♔b4 ♘e5 6 ♘xe5 fxe5 7 ♔xa4 e4 8 ♔b5 ♔d7 9 ♖c3 ♖e8 10 b7 ♔d6 11 ♖c8 and Black resigned.

Page 117 (top diagram): No, because after 1 ♖xh6 ♔g7, the white rook is trapped. White should play 1 ♖h8+, escaping before the trap closes.

Page 117 (bottom diagram): At first sight Black cannot promote a pawn, because after 1...b4 2 axb4 axb4 3 ♔e2, White's king catches the black pawn. However, Black can be more cunning: after 1...b4 2 axb4, he should play 2...a4 and now his passed pawn is one square further away from White's king, and so White cannot catch the pawn. If White pushes his own pawn by 3 b5, then Black can either play 3...a3 followed by promoting with check, or 3...♔e7 stopping White's pawn with his king.

Page 118 (top diagram): White's attack strikes home first after 1 ♖h8+ ♔xh8 2 ♕h5+ ♔g8 3 ♕h7+ ♔f8 4 ♕h8 checkmate. The rook sacrifice gives White's queen the chance to enter the attack with check, so Black never gets time to finish off his own attack.

Page 118 (middle diagram): A quick one-two picks up a piece with 1 ♕a4+ (double attack) 1...♘c6 (the only way to counter the check and defend the bishop on b4) 2 ♗xc6+ (destroying the guard) 2...bxc6 3 ♕xb4 and White has won a piece.

Page 118 (bottom diagram): White can win a pawn by temporarily sacrificing a piece to set up a double attack: 1 ♗xh7+ ♔xh7 2 ♕c2+ ♔g8 3 ♕xc6, and White regains the sacrificed piece. The net result is that Black has lost his pawn on h7.

Page 119 (top diagram): At the moment Black's king and queen are not lined up for a skewer, but after 1 ♕g5+ Black has no choice but to play 1...♔e6, and then 2 ♕g8+ wins Black's queen.

Page 119 (middle diagram): White wins by 1 ♕g5+. At first sight this may appear to be a blunder, because of Black's bishop on f6. But this bishop is pinned against the king, so it cannot take the white queen. It follows that Black must move his king, and then White can take the bishop with either bishop or queen, winning a piece.

Page 119 (bottom diagram): The best way of meeting the check is to take the rook with the bishop on h6. This may appear obvious, but it is easy to miss a long backward move, especially if the board is crowded with pieces.

Page 120 (top diagram): White can create a double attack by playing 1 ♘g5. This not only threatens 2 ♗xb7, but also 2 ♕xh7 checkmate. Black has nothing better than to play 1...♗xg5, and after 2 ♗xb7 the rook in the corner is trapped, so White will win a rook in return for a bishop. This idea is a combination of two motifs: combined attack and trapping a piece.

Page 120 (middle diagram): White can force checkmate in two moves by a spectacular queen sacrifice: 1 ♕xh7+ ♚xh7 2 ♖h4 checkmate. Notice that playing 1 ♖h4 first doesn't work, because Black can defend by 1...♘xf6.

Page 120 (bottom diagram): White can win material by 1 ♘c6+, forcing Black to move his king, and then 2 ♘e7, forking the two black rooks. White ends up winning a rook (worth five points) in return for a knight (worth three points).

Page 121 (top diagram): White can win material using a discovered attack. The key move is 1 ♗b4, attacking the rook on f8 directly, and also discovering an attack on Black's queen. Black has to deal with the attack on the queen by moving her, and then White can take the rook, winning a rook in return for a bishop.

Page 121 (middle diagram): White can win a pawn by exploiting the bad position of Black's king. The best move is 1 ♕xa7, simply stealing Black's pawn. Black cannot play 1...♖xa7, because White would reply 2 ♖d8 mate, so White has simply made off with a useful pawn.

Page 121 (bottom diagram): White can win a piece by playing 1 ♗xd7. If Black recaptures with the knight by 1...♘xd7, then 2 ♗xd8 takes the queen. On the other hand, 1...♛xd7 removes a defender from the knight on f6, and White wins a piece by 2 ♝xf6. Black is in a no-win situation and must lose material.

Page 122 (top diagram): Incredibly, White can trap Black's queen by 1 ♖a1. Wherever the queen moves, White can win it, for example 1...♛xa1 2 ♘b3+ with a knight fork, 1...♛e4 2 ♖a4+ with a skewer, 1...♛d5 2 ♖d1+ with another skewer, or 1...♛a8 2 ♘b3+ with a discovered attack – most of the tactics mentioned under Rule 6 rolled up in one position!

Page 122 (middle position): White can force checkmate in three by sacrificing his queen: 1 ♛g7+ ♚xg7 2 ♘f5++ ♚g8 3 ♘h6 checkmate. Notice that White's second move was a *double check* from both bishop and knight. A double check is one of the most forcing moves available in chess, because *a double check can only be met by a king move.*

Page 122 (bottom diagram): The last position is a bit of fun after the rest of the book. Here White can win with a kind of cascading knight fork, but to set it up he must first sacrifice his queen: 1 ♛a8+ ♚xa8 2 ♘xb6+ ♚b8 3 ♘xd7+ and then 4 ♘xf8. The white knight single-handedly annihilates the entire enemy army.